Praise for *Letting Go of Nothing*

"Peter Russell is like a friend who offers us a cool drink of water on a hot day. *Letting Go of Nothing* invites us to pause, step back, and see if there is another way of seeing that allows the mind to relax its grip and for a natural letting go to happen. Wise, eloquent, and subtle."

— **John J. Prendergast, PhD**, author of
The Deep Heart and *In Touch*

"Cuts right through to the essence of what is important for us to live a content, joyful life, waking up to who we truly are and being able to make meaningful contributions. I heartily recommend this book to anyone looking for more peace in their life and for anyone wanting to wake up. Enjoy!"

— **Lama Palden Drolma**, author of *Love on Every Breath*

"*Letting Go of Nothing* is a marvelously simple, clear, and concise guide to discovering the freedom and peace of mind that are right here. In plain language, Peter Russell illuminates a lifelong, moment-to-moment path of seeing how we create unnecessary suffering and waking up to the unfettered wonder of simple presence. This book is practical, wise, warmhearted, and refreshingly down-to-earth. I recommend it very highly."

— **Joan Tollifson**, author of *Nothing to Grasp*
and *Death: The End of Self-Improvement*

"Seven centuries ago, Meister Eckhart, one of the greatest Christian contemplatives, decided 'to find which is the greatest and best virtue.' He concluded that it is letting go of cravings, and around the world and across the centuries thousands of sages have echoed this theme. Now, in an era that desperately needs this skill, Peter Russell provides us with a simple, lucid guide to the importance of letting go and how to do it."

— **Roger Walsh, MD, PhD**, University of California Medical
School, author of *Essential Spirituality*

"In this insightful book, Peter Russell takes us on a personal journey in which he reveals what life has taught him about being human. Each of the short chapters contains a peek into his own awakening journey, where we are reminded that what seems to create a life of happiness and fulfillment has little to do with one's outer circumstances but rather with our openness to the *is-ness* of each moment. This is more than a book about finding inner peace — though it is that, for sure. It is also a book about human possibilities."

— **Susan Campbell, PhD**, author of
Getting Real and *From Triggered to Tranquil*

"This book expresses the essence of spiritual wisdom without excess baggage. It is a clear glass of water, a refreshing simplicity. In it, Peter Russell has given elegant expression to what stands forth when we let go into what is, without resistance or confusion. Enjoy it, and may you find it easier and more natural to keep letting go into the spacious beauty of what is, here and now."

— **Terry Patten**, author of *Integral Life Practice*
and *A New Republic of the Heart*

"*Letting Go of Nothing* is at once a wise yet completely practical distillation of the many avenues available to all who are searching for peace, love, and contentment by living a more awakened life. Each chapter is concise and continually points the reader to our true nature while also humbly and wholeheartedly accepting the challenges of our human expressions. Peter Russell writes with a profound directness and simplicity wrought from his own experience. Here is a book that is, indeed, 'bringing awakening down to earth.'"

— **Dorothy Hunt**, spiritual teacher, author of *Ending the Search*

"People in Western societies are besotted with the concept of being in control at all times in all ways. This chronic uptightness leaves nothing to chance and the flowing ways of nature. In *Letting Go of Nothing*, Peter Russell shows that in order to be happier and achieve more, we must embrace the paradox of letting go. As Russell shows, this is not new-age pop psychology but ancient wisdom. It endures for one reason: it works."

— **Larry Dossey, MD**, author of *One Mind*

"The realization that we are not our thoughts is a gateway to liberation. *Letting Go of Nothing* offers wise guidance and inspiration, pointing to the deep peace and freedom that arise naturally in moments of letting be."

— **Tara Brach**, author of
Radical Acceptance and *Radical Compassion*

"This book not only makes a clear case for why unhappiness is *not* intrinsic to human nature but provides a roadmap from our stuck point to the destination — a sense of self-control and freedom from the prison of chronic unrest. Why would anyone not integrate this straightforward and profoundly effective technology of mind to create a radically transformed life?"

— **Barbara Fields, LHD**, executive director
of the Association for Global New Thought

"This book reads like the distilled wisdom of a whole lifetime of inner exploration, expressed with great clarity and simplicity. You can read the book sequentially, or open chapters at random, and you will be enriched and enlightened by what you find."

— **Steve Taylor**, author of
The Clear Light and *Extraordinary Awakenings*

"I have long appreciated the writings of Peter Russell and his eagerness to bring the spiritual and the scientific together. In this book he invites us into his soul and value system, his application of meditation and Buddhist practice to his own way of seeing the world and self, and in doing so he summons us to 'the deep peace of our true nature.' I, too, take hope, and Peter Russell's book

affirms it, that our species will wake up to the down-to-earth spiritual wisdom that all our religions, when healthy, call us to — keeping it simple, understandable, and effective so that we and the sacred planet we share might become sustainable once more."
— **Matthew Fox**, author of *Meister Eckhart* and other books

"In *Letting Go of Nothing*, Peter Russell has distilled the essence of the traditional path of surrender into clear, simple, accessible language. Every short chapter contains both a unique insight and a pathway that, if followed in one's own experience, will lead directly to the peace that 'passeth all understanding.' Short enough to be read in a weekend, profound enough to last a lifetime, *Letting Go of Nothing* is a gem of contemporary spirituality."
— **Rupert Spira**, author and teacher

"*Letting Go of Nothing* is a clear, engaging book filled with deep wisdom that presents the heart of the Buddha's teachings in a down-to-earth, highly user-friendly way. This beautiful, jargon-free guide shows how to free the mind of its self-created prison. If the reader puts these teachings into practice, they will definitely find support for genuine liberation."
— **James Baraz**, author of *Awakening Joy* and cofounder of Spirit Rock Meditation Center

LETTING GO
of NOTHING

ALSO BY PETER RUSSELL

The Brain Book
The Consciousness Revolution
The Creative Manager
From Science to God
The Global Brain
The TM Technique
The Upanishads: A New Translation with Alistair Shearer
Waking Up in Time

• An Eckhart Tolle Edition •

LETTING GO
of NOTHING

Relax Your Mind and Discover
the Wonder of Your True Nature

PETER RUSSELL

FOREWORD BY ECKHART TOLLE

New World Library
Novato, California

An Eckhart Tolle Edition
www.eckharttolle.com

New World Library
14 Pamaron Way
Novato, California 94949

Text design by Megan Colman and Tona Pearce Myers

Library of Congress Cataloging-in-Publication Data

Names: Russell, Peter, date, author.
Title: Letting go of nothing : relax your mind and discover the wonder of your true nature / Peter Russell ; foreword by Eckhart Tolle.
Description: Novato : New World Library, 2021. | Summary: "Describes the spiritual practice of 'letting go' — surrendering our attachments to people, things, expectations, and even our own opinions. The author shows how this practice, recognized in both Western and Eastern spiritual traditions, leads to a greater sense of peace and openness to life as it is"-- Provided by publisher.
Identifiers: LCCN 2021017427 (print) | LCCN 2021017428 (ebook) | ISBN 9781608687657 (hardcover) | ISBN 9781608687664 (epub)
Subjects: LCSH: Asceticism. | Healing--Psychological aspects. | Mental healing. | Self-realization. | Forgiveness.
Classification: LCC BL625 .R87 2021 (print) | LCC BL625 (ebook) | DDC 204/.47--dc23
LC record available at https://lccn.loc.gov/2021017427
LC ebook record available at https://lccn.loc.gov/2021017428

First printing, August 2021
ISBN 978-1-60868-765-7
Ebook ISBN 978-1-60868-766-4
Printed in the USA on 30% postconsumer-waste recycled paper

New World Library is proud to be a Gold Certified Environmentally Responsible Publisher. Publisher certification awarded by Green Press Initiative.

10   9   8   7   6   5   4   3   2

If you let go a little, you have a little peace.
If you let go a lot, you have a lot of peace.
If you let go completely, you have complete peace.

— AJAHN CHAH

CONTENTS

FOREWORD

SINCE ANCIENT TIMES, the practice of letting go has been recognized in both Eastern and Western religious traditions as a prerequisite for self-transcendence and spiritual awakening. It was usually equated with giving up all the things the egoic self derives its sustenance from. The sadhus (ascetic mendicants) of India, the Islamic Sufis, and the Buddhist monastics all shared this practice, as did some ancient Greek philosophers such as Diogenes and the early Christian hermits known as the Desert Fathers and Mothers, whose lifestyle and practice evolved into the monastic tradition of the Middle Ages.

They all held the belief that to make any progress on the spiritual path, we need to give up everything the worldly self could attach itself to and feed on: first and foremost our material possessions but also our home, rich food, comfort, sexuality, personal relationships, and all pleasures of the senses. The idea behind it was that these practices would deprive the ego or false self of anything it could identify with, thus starving it to death, so to speak. The idea is by no means as absurd as it might appear to us in the twenty-first century, and some of these intrepid explorers of the inner realms, so it seems, did indeed attain self-transcendence and realized "the peace that passeth all understanding," to use the words of the Bible.

It is safe to say, however, that the vast majority of them remained confined in their egoic sense of self. Many would identify with their religious belief structures, which is to say ideologies, and mistake them for "the Truth that makes you free." Others developed a strong self-image based on their perceived spiritual status as humans who have renounced everything. In other words, the ego was able to sneak in again through the back door, as it were. Without realizing it, these spiritual practitioners had found themselves trapped again in a conceptual identity. Most of them tended to place excessive emphasis on letting go of externals, thus neglecting the inner aspect of letting go. One could say that, seemingly paradoxically, they let go of everything but failed to let go of no-thing.

Peter Russell's invaluable book can become an essential companion on your spiritual path. It clearly shows the importance of the inner dimension of letting go, the letting go of attachment to thought as well as to emotions, which are the reflections of thought. These thought forms are narratives that become a dense veil through which we perceive, or rather misperceive, reality. These narratives — the voices in the head — may consist of expectations, complaints, regrets, grievances, worry, and so on. Many narratives, especially the repetitive ones, generate anxiety, anger, hatred, and other negative emotions. These narratives constitute what we might call the unobserved mind. This unobserved mind is responsible for most of the human-made suffering on the planet, both personal and collective.

Most humans are still, almost literally, possessed by thought. They don't think, but thinking happens to them. The beginning of spiritual awakening is the realization that you are not the voice in your head but the one who is aware of the voice. You are the awareness behind your thoughts. As this realization grows, you begin to derive your sense of identity increasingly from the space of awareness rather than from the narratives in your mind. You are *letting go of the identification with thought*. Thought is no longer imbued with self!

That is the ultimate letting go, the only true renunciation. You are still able to enjoy external things such as possessions and sensory pleasures, but they lose their overriding importance and their addictive nature. You enjoy them with a sense of detachment, while they last. (Spoiler alert: they won't last!) You don't seek yourself in them anymore. Life sheds its absolute seriousness.

I suggest you use this book as a manual for this inner letting go, the primary spiritual practice. What is the criterion for progress on this path? Thought increasingly loses its capacity to make you unhappy! You are less reactive in the face of challenging situations or people. You recognize worry as futile and destructive, so you are able to let it go when it happens. You find inner peace and contentment in the present moment. And perhaps you begin to realize that you are not a person but an essential and intrinsic part of the evolution of universal consciousness.

—— ECKHART TOLLE

PREFACE

THE CALL TO LET GO lies at the heart of the world's spiritual traditions. Not being attached to outcomes, surrendering desires, accepting the present, opening to a higher power, relinquishing the ego, practicing forgiveness — all entail letting go.

Why is letting go deemed so important? Holding on, these teachings repeatedly affirm, limits our perception, clouds our thinking, and lies behind much of our suffering.

Letting go, on the other hand, brings relief. The mind relaxes, and free from tension and the energy that went into holding on, we feel more at ease. We see things as they are without any overlay of fear or anxiety. We are more open to others, and to love. We realize that what we were seeking by holding on — safety, happiness, joy, peace of mind — was there all along. But our holding on veiled its presence.

Letting go can take many forms: letting go of fixed beliefs or points of view, letting go of being right, letting go of ego, letting go of the past or expectations of the future, letting go of attachments to possessions or relationships, letting go of judgments and grievances, letting go of unhealthy emotions, letting go of assumptions about how things should or should not be.

In these and many other instances, we are being called to let go of beliefs, projections, expectations, interpretations, attitudes, and attachments. These aren't *things* in the way that objects like a book, a house, or a person are. They exist only in the mind.

We are not letting go of things themselves as much as the way we see them. Hence the title of this book: *Letting Go of Nothing*. Or, as I sometimes like to put it, "Letting Go of No-Thing."

᠅

THE SEEDS OF THE BOOK were sown long ago. When I first learned to meditate, I realized how valuable letting go could be — even if not always easy. In the late sixties and early seventies I had the good fortunate to study with Maharishi Mahesh Yogi, the founder of Transcendental Meditation. He emphasized complete effortlessness, letting go of trying to achieve some special state. Through his teachings I gained a grounding in Indian philosophy and the nature of spiritual awakening that became the foundation for much of my work back then. And it still is.

Later, the book *A Course in Miracles* crossed my path. Its essential message could be summed up as the need to let go of the ego's thought system. It offered a variety of exercises and meditations to that end, which resonated with what I was discovering and deepened my practice.

Over time, I became increasingly familiar with the Buddha's teachings. He saw that holding on to our attachments to what will make us happy is the primary cause of suffering. Thus we can free ourselves from suffering by letting go of grasping, letting go of our ideas about how things should be, our desires, our fears, and our aversions.

More recently, contemporary teachers such as Rupert Spira, Francis Lucille, Eckhart Tolle, and Ram Dass have helped clarify my thinking and approach. The reader who is familiar with any of these traditions or teachings will probably detect their influence on the following pages. But as far as possible I've endeavored to write from my own understanding and experience. My explanations reflect the way I make sense of the subject, and the practices I suggest are ones that work for me. I offer them in the hope they will be of help in your own journey of awakening.

A CHANGE *of* MIND

I JUST COULDN'T LET GO. Nothing I tried seemed to work.

For two days I'd been resenting my partner. She wanted it her way, and I wanted it mine. It was one of those squabbles that occurs from time to time in any relationship. I felt justified in my position and frustrated with her. And she, no doubt, felt the same way about me. It wasn't that big an issue but enough to leave some tension in the air.

I tried to let it go, telling myself it didn't really matter, that it would all blow over soon enough. I tried to forget it, or at least not to carp on about it anymore. I tried to shift my feelings. But it didn't work. Inside, I still felt resentful. And it was souring our relationship.

Later, I was sitting at my desk working on a project but still distracted by the issue. I knew the problem lay in how I was seeing things, but I remained stuck. Then I thought to simply ask, *Is there another way of seeing this?* I was not trying to come up with an answer but just posing the question and seeing what happened.

Almost instantly, everything changed. I saw my partner

as another human being with her own history, her own needs and preferences, doing the best she could to navigate her way through life. I saw her through the eyes of compassion rather than grievance and judgment. For two days I'd been out of love, but now the love returned. My jaw relaxed, my belly softened, and I felt at ease again.

It all felt so obvious. Why hadn't I seen this before? How could I have become so fixated in my self-righteous point of view?

I had wanted my partner to change, but what actually needed to change was my mind. That couldn't happen as long as I was holding on to a grievance. I had to pause, step back, and then pose the question, with an open, curious attitude, *Could there, just possibly, be another way of seeing this?* without trying to find an answer or even assuming there was an answer. My inner knowing was then able to shine through and reveal another more helpful way of seeing things.

Only then, in the light of this new perspective, could my mind release its grip. Letting go then happened spontaneously — without any effort on my part.

LETTING GO IS HARD *to* DO

IF LETTING GO IS SO VALUABLE, why don't we just do it?

The answer, as we all know from experience, is that letting go is not as easy as it sounds.

After the death of a beloved animal companion, for example, friends may see our distress and say something like, "You just have to let go." Something similar can happen after a devastating relationship breakup. People say, "Just move on." And while these suggestions may be correct in a way, they are not so helpful because "just letting go" under such conditions can be extremely difficult. The memory of such a painful loss still strikes us to the core, no matter our intentions.

The difficulty stems from treating letting go as another thing to do. But we can't "do" letting go, however hard we try. To let go, we have to cease the "doing" of holding on. And that requires a quite different approach.

Imagine you are holding a small rock in the air. Holding on takes effort, which keeps the muscles of your hand tense. To let go, we relax our muscles and release our grip. We cease holding on, and letting go happens.

It works similarly with the mind. Here the grip we need to release is a mental one — our holding on to some attitude, belief, expectation, or judgment. We need to allow our minds to relax — literally, "to be loose again."

So we should approach letting go not as another thing to do, but as *un-doing* the holding on. It is not trying in any way; instead, it's developing the internal conditions that help the mind relax, allowing the letting go to happen.

Although this may sound unconventional — and it certainly does entail a very different approach from the frustrating trying to let go we easily default to — I have found it to be a far more effective path. In the following pages I will explain how it works and introduce various approaches to letting go that I have found helpful. They are all based on reframing letting go as "letting in" and "letting be."

LETTING IN

THE FIRST STEP IN LETTING GO is to *let in*. Initially, this may sound counterintuitive. We assume that letting go of something means getting rid of it, pushing it away. If we want to let go of some grievance, we may try not to think about what the other person did and how awful they were. Or if we want to let go of our attachment to money, we may try to stop worrying about our finances, pushing such concerns to the back of our mind. However, the central idea of this book is that we should do the opposite. In order to release the grip our mind has on some attitude or idea, we first need to *let in* the experience of holding on. If we are not aware we are holding on to a rock, we cannot let our grip relax.

To let in an experience means to allow it more fully into awareness, to become curious about what is going on. Let's take as an example some bodily discomfort or tension. You may already be aware of discomfort somewhere in the body. If not, be curious whether there might be something you haven't noticed. Some sensation may then reveal itself. It was probably on the edge of your awareness, but because your attention was focused on reading the book or some other experience, you didn't notice it. Innocent curiosity opens you to the possibility that you might have missed something, giving it the opportunity to enter your awareness.

When you do notice physical discomfort somewhere, let it in, be curious about how it feels. It might appear as tightness, a muscle ache, or a feeling of pressure somewhere. How far does it spread? Is it localized or more diffuse? The key is opening your awareness to what is rather than trying to change anything.

We can apply the same principles to more painful experiences that may initially seem much harder to let in. We tend to turn our attention away from pain, distracting ourselves with some task, becoming numb to it, or resorting to painkillers to get rid of (or at least subdue) the pain. We fear that if we let the pain in, it will hurt more. And that's the last thing we want.

Yet pain calls for the very opposite. Pain evolved to alert organisms to bodily damage or dysfunction. It is meant to be unpleasant. It is a call for attention, the body's alarm bell: *Hey! There's something wrong here. Attention, please.* Rather than ignoring it, resisting it, or trying to make it go away, we can give pain the attention it is requesting.

If we follow this call, and open up to the pain — taking the risk of letting in how it feels — we may find it does at first seem stronger, just as we feared. But as we explore it more, becoming interested in what is actually there, we find that what we had labeled as a pain or an ache now becomes more specific, perhaps a sharpness here or a tightness there; maybe it's a sense of pressure, a stinging, a prickling, or some other sensation.

AND LETTING BE

HAVING LET THE SENSATION IN, the second part of letting go is *letting be*. Don't try to change the feelings that have appeared or wish they weren't there. Instead, accept them as they are. Let your attention stay with them in an innocent, curious way, almost as if you were experiencing them for the first time. Think of it as making friends with the sensations, getting to know them.

As you do, you may notice it doesn't feel as bad as you thought it would and might become a little easier to be with.

Pain, it is often said, is inevitable; suffering is optional. The pain is the physical sensation. The suffering, on the other hand, comes from our aversion to the pain, our wishing it weren't there. It is an added layer of discomfort that results from not accepting what is, from holding on to our idea of how things should be. But in the present moment, if there is pain, it's real, it's there. Resisting the pain doesn't help; it only adds to the discomfort. By accepting it as it is, allowing the sensations to be just as they are, we may well find we don't suffer quite so much.

As you let the experience in and let it be, you might notice that it begins to change, sometimes in unexpected ways, and without any effort on your part. A sharp sensation might soften. An ache might grow stronger, and then fade. Numbness might give way to other sensations. A tense muscle might begin to unwind of its own accord.

The body knows which muscles are tense and how that tension is held in place. It knows what needs to be released. But most of this information never reaches the conscious mind; we don't know exactly what needs to be released, or how to release it. However, if we become aware of the tension and experience how it feels without trying to reject it, we open a door for the body's innate wisdom to shine through.

Sometimes when I am sitting for a long period, I feel a pain beneath one of my shoulder blades. I recognize that it probably has something to do with my posture, but despite readjusting my position to relieve the pain, it keeps returning. My conscious mind cannot sort it out.

But if I open up to it more fully — letting it in and then just letting it be — the natural wisdom of my body often shows me what needs to happen. Several muscles that I did not realize were tight begin to relax, the area softens, and my body readjusts itself. Without my doing anything, the pain goes and comfort returns. The body does the releasing for me — once, that is, my conscious mind gets out of the way.

Werner Erhard taught a similar process in est — Erhard Seminar Training — a pioneering program of the 1970s human potential movement. He would ask people to describe a pain in terms of its shape, size, color, and texture and to rate each on a scale from 1 to 10. He'd then ask them to go through the process again, rating how it now felt. As they continued repeating the process, the intensity of the pain would tend to decrease, often disappearing completely. By using these sensory metaphors, people were opening up more to the feeling of the pain. They were, in effect, letting it in and letting it be.

In other situations, where the pain has some deeper, long-term cause, it may not go away, but our relationship to it can change, making it easier to bear. A woman I heard of had severe pain, caused by bone spurs along the spinal column. She was in continuous pain for years before she discovered her meditation practice, which allowed her to relax around the pain and open up to it. She reported that this letting in brought welcome relief from the debilitating effects of the pain. The pain hadn't changed, but her relationship to it had, dramatically.

I don't mean to imply we should always take this approach to pain. There may be times when turning our attention away is the appropriate response, and sometimes taking a painkiller might be just what we need. Or, as is often the case, we may need to look for the cause of the pain and do whatever is necessary to remedy it.

I have even found the principle of letting in and letting be helpful in situations where there is no obvious discomfort and little reason to suspect I'm holding on. There was a time when I was exploring ways to relax more fully before going to sleep at night. Lying there in bed, I might not feel any obvious tension; indeed, my body would seem quite relaxed. Adopting the principle of open curiosity, I'd wonder if perhaps I was still holding on somewhere. I'd simply pose the question, in an open way, much as I did in the earlier example of the upset with my partner: *Could there be some tension I'm not aware of? Does my body want to show me something?* I would not look for anything but just remain open to the possibility, waiting to see if anything revealed itself.

After a while, I'd usually notice an area begin to soften slightly. As I stayed with the sensations, allowing the softening to continue, I'd find muscles that I thought were already relaxed beginning to relax even more. Then my body might spontaneously adjust its position a little in response to the increased relaxation. Other muscle groups followed, as my whole body sank into a deeper relaxation.

And before I knew it, I was asleep.

WHAT DO YOU WANT?

BEFORE GOING FURTHER into different ways of letting go, let's first explore what lies behind our holding on. Why do we cling to our beliefs and theories, our judgments and grievances, our feelings and our stories? Why do we become so attached to our possessions, our self-image, and what we think will make us happy?

To answer that, we should first ask, *What do we want?*

Ask the proverbial person on the street what they want, and you might get answers such as: a better-paying job, a healthier body, a meaningful relationship, a more spacious home, a good vacation, reconnecting with an old friend, or some special treat. Dig deeper and ask why they want these things, and you will hear responses such as: to be loved and appreciated, to feel safe, to be in closer community, to be stimulated.

But why do we want these things? What is the underlying motivation? Again, answers may vary: pleasure, happiness, contentment, peace of mind, enjoyment, fulfillment, ease. Notice a common theme here? All these answers point to a better state of mind.

This is the fundamental drive behind all our needs. We seek security because it makes us feel better. We want physical comforts so we can relax and be at ease. We enjoy having mental stimulation and emotional nourishment. We are happier if we have a positive self-image and others approve of us. It feels good to love and be loved.

The gratification need not be immediate. Most of us do not enjoy visiting the dentist, but we go hoping to avoid more pain later. Or we may forgo some personal gain and help another in need because we feel the better for it. Even the masochist who sets out to cause himself pain does so because he derives some satisfaction from it.

This is our true bottom line: a better state of mind.

When we hear the term *bottom line*, we usually think of money: How much profit is there? How much does it cost? But money is not our ultimate bottom line. It is merely the means to buy the things, opportunities, experiences, or whatever else we think will make us happy. The fundamental criterion, conscious or unconscious, behind all our decisions is: *Will I feel better for it? Will I be happier, more content, more at ease?*

We may think we seek some external goal, but in truth we seek it hoping that, in one way or another, we will feel better inside.

As the Dalai Lama once remarked, "In the final analysis, the hope of every person is simply peace of mind."

RETURNING *to* NATURAL MIND

IT MIGHT SOUND HEDONISTIC to say that we're all seeking happiness. But it is completely natural — a self-centeredness in service of our biological survival.

When there are no imminent threats to our well-being, when our needs are met and we have nothing to worry about, we feel relaxed and at ease. This is the mind in its natural unperturbed state, untarnished by complaints, desires, or worries. I call it *natural mind*.

By natural I do not mean "normal." Normal means the norm or the average. A normal state of mind would be what most people experience most of the time — which, for the vast majority, is *not* relaxed and at ease. I am speaking of the mind before it is sullied by wants and fears. It is how we feel when we're not threatened or worried. Put simply, when everything is OK in our world, we feel OK inside.

When, on the other hand, some need or threat arises, the contentment of natural mind is replaced by feelings of discontent. The feelings associated with being cold or hungry, for example, are not so pleasant: indeed, if we are extremely cold or hungry, the experience can be painful. And so it should be. To feel at ease in a dangerous situation could jeopardize our survival.

Discomfort, pain, and suffering are intrinsically unpleasant experiences. They are a call for attention, telling us that something needs taking care of. So if we're cold, we warm ourselves by moving closer to a fire, and if we're hungry we eat something. Once the need has been satisfied or the danger averted, the mind returns to its natural state of contentment. All is well again.

One might expect there to be a natural alternation between these two modes of functioning: the open, relaxed awareness of natural mind, on the one hand, interspersed with periods of discontent arising from some imminent need or threat, on the other — ideally, spending most of our time in a contented state.

Other animals manage this easily enough. A dog with nothing to do will sit and watch the world go by, pricking its ears at a sound of potential interest. Then, if everything is OK, it will relax again. But human beings are different. We set ourselves apart from just about every other creature by spending most of our time in discontent.

Why is this? Why are we so seldom content? One would think that we humans — with all our understanding of the world and the many technologies we've invented to change it — would have taken care of our needs and banished most potential threats. We should be even more contented than our pets. Where did we go wrong?

AN INNOVATIVE SPECIES

HUMAN BEINGS' UNIQUE ABILITY to create a better world for themselves stems from three major evolutionary developments.

In just a few million years — a mere blink in evolutionary time — our ancestors' brains tripled in size. Areas responsible for planning, decision-making, and social awareness all grew rapidly, along with areas involved with cognition and the processing of language.

The facial muscles and the larynx also changed, allowing our ancestors to make the complex sounds needed for speech. All animals learn from experience, but with speech, humans could learn not only from their own experiences but also from those of others. They could tell each other what they had seen, heard, or discovered and so build up a collective body of knowledge, far greater than any one individual ever could.

Speech meant not only that people could talk to each other but also that they could talk to themselves, in their own minds — the essence of what we commonly call "thinking." Thinking allowed them to identify patterns in their experience, form concepts, and make generalizations. They could apply reason, understand the world, decide on alternative courses of action, and make plans.

However, before all this could be put to good use, they needed to be able to turn those plans into action. This is where another unique feature came into play: the human hand. Or to be more precise, the fully opposable thumb, which turned the hand into a most elegant and versatile organ with which to manipulate the world.

Combine this power to change things with a growing body of knowledge and the ability to think, reason, and make choices, and you have a creature able to mold the clay of Mother Earth into a diversity of new forms.

We learned to make edges on stones, giving us axes, knives, and points to our spears. We built shelters for ourselves; we made clothes. We tamed fire, which helped keep us warm, cook food, and later, smelt metals. We developed agriculture, sowed seeds, and irrigated the land. We invented the wheel, developed new modes of transport, found new sources of energy, and created new materials. And we invented better and better tools with which to do all these things. We've amplified the power inherent in the human hand into technologies that can change the world in ways that would have been unimaginable to our ancestors.

The opposable thumb had one other crucial significance: it made writing possible, allowing us to record the wealth of knowledge we were gaining. And we did not stop at writing; we progressed to printing, then the telephone, radio, television, computers, and the internet.

Behind all these developments lay a recurrent theme. We wanted to live longer and healthier lives; we sought to reduce pain and suffering; we wanted to create a world in which we felt safe and secure. We wanted to feel more at ease and content. To be happy. We may not have been aware of it, but we were seeking ways to return to natural mind.

And yet, despite all our advances, things haven't worked out as well as we might have hoped. Are people in the developed world any happier than the Yanomami Indians in the Brazilian rain forest or the Sentinelese of the Andaman Islands — two cultures until recently largely untainted by the modern world?

Are we any happier today than we were fifty years ago? A study in 1955 found that one-third of the adult US population were happy with their lives. The same study repeated thirty-five years later found that the number of people happy with their lives had not changed — despite the fact that per capita productivity and consumption had both doubled over this time.

So why, despite all this progress, are we still not happy? The answer lies in another factor essential to our creativity — imagination.

IMAGINED REALITIES

THE WORD *imagination* means literally the ability to "make images" in the mind. This includes not just visual images but other sensory modalities — sounds, smells, tastes, textures, feelings. Our thoughts, too, appear in the mind, most commonly as a voice in the head, conversations we have with ourselves.

Thoughts may also trigger other mental images. I can have the idea of a sunset, say, and then see a mental picture of one. I can think of the opening lines of Beethoven's Fifth Symphony, the chorus of "All You Need Is Love," or some other familiar piece of music and hear it in my mind. Or I can think of a foreign city and then imagine what it would be like to walk down its streets. I can even imagine something impossible (or highly improbable) such as a pink elephant or a humpback whale in the desert speaking Japanese.

Thinking expanded our relationship to time. We can think about an earlier time (what we did last weekend, for example) and trigger a variety of memories. In our imagination, we can relive the story of our own lives, learning from it, sometimes rejoicing, sometimes grieving. And we can go back even further, beyond our own memory. We can imagine people and events that came before us; we can go back in time to earlier generations, to our ancestors, and to what came before them. We can even imagine how life itself, and even the Universe, might have begun.

We can also think about the future, imagining what we will eat for dinner, where we'll go tomorrow, or our next vacation. We can speculate about what might happen, plan ahead, and make decisions about situations that may not occur for many years. And we can imagine how the world might be long after we are gone.

Imagination adds a whole new dimension to reality. Our primary reality is our immediate sensory experience: what we see, hear, taste, smell, touch, and feel in the present. The world of our imagination — thoughts, memories, possible futures — all exist in a parallel secondary reality.

To call imagination a "reality" may at first sound strange. We tend to think of the physical world as real and of what goes on in the mind as not real. There is some truth in this insofar as the objective reality of our senses is something we can all observe and largely agree on. Imagination is subjective and private and in that respect is not part of the real world we see "out there." On the other hand, our subjective experience is very real to us. The dreams we have at night are real at the time. They may be created from memory rather than present sensory experience and influenced by unconscious needs and motivations, but they are real enough to make us fearful or excited, raise our heart rate, or bring out a sweat. Memories of our childhood, or images of our next vacation, are real experiences. So, too, are our thoughts; they may exist only in the mind, but there they are real.

Both realities — our experience of the present and the world of our imagination — can coexist, and do so much of the time. I may see a bud on a bush and, in my mind, remember its name and imagine what the flower will look like when the bud opens. Or, driving down a street, I may see traffic ahead and begin picturing alternate routes.

Being able to live in both realities is intrinsic to being human and, most important, plays an essential role in creativity and innovation. Everything we have created, from the wheel to the internet, began in someone's imagination.

Innovation — literally "bringing in the new" — starts as insights, ideas, or images in the mind. In our imagination we assess the situation, play out scenarios, choose alternatives, plan next steps, and so forth. And then, when we've decided on a course of action, we bring the new into the world.

But imagination also comes with a cost. It can be so engrossing it eclipses our experience of the present moment. It may start as a little thought bubble. Perhaps we wonder what the weather will be like tomorrow. We recall hearing that rain is in the forecast. We start thinking about where we have to go, what it might be like there. What will we need to take? How will we feel? Should we change our plans? Within a short time, this initially innocuous thought bubble has become a full-blown alternate reality. Our attention becomes absorbed in tomorrow's world, and the present moment recedes into the background.

We are, literally, lost in thought. Entranced by our

imagined worlds, we lose awareness of our self in the here and now.

To make matters worse, our imagined realities often trigger unnecessary and unwelcome emotions. We become fearful of potential misfortunes. We worry over whether we will make the right decision. Or we obsess about situations over which we have no direct influence.

As Mark Twain famously remarked, "I am an old man and have known a great many troubles, but most of them never happened."

DECONSTRUCTING *an* EMOTION

THE WORD *emotion* comes from the Latin *emovere*, meaning "to move out." It was originally used in the sense of an agitation or a stirring up of the mind. Anger is certainly a stirring up of the mind, as are grief, frustration, sadness, excitement, and desire. Emotions such as these perturb the mind, taking us out of our natural state of ease.

There is a second sense in which emotions are a "moving out." Most emotions stem from some call to action. Whether it's an urge to fight that may arise with anger, a pulling back that comes with fear, or an impulse to bond in sexual attraction, an emotion is an impulse to act, to move out in some way. Even the inclination to withdraw that can come with depression, sadness, or shame can be considered a form of action.

With the impulse to move, the brain sends signals to relevant muscles, preparing them for action. When we feel anger, we may clench our fists and perhaps grit our teeth. With fear, we may experience a quivering sensation in our body as it prepares to run. Or with shame, we may have an urge to withdraw and hide.

Because we are socialized animals, we seldom act out these impulses. Unlike a dog, which may snap at someone if it feels threatened or chase a cat the moment it sees one, we usually hold back. Obviously, this is a good thing socially. Otherwise we'd all be fighting, running away, or making love at every opportunity.

But this restraint can also be to our detriment. If the impulse to act is not followed through, the body can stay in a state of preparedness long after the trigger has passed, leaving a residue of tension. And if another emotional reaction gets triggered before this one has abated, tensions may accumulate, leading to a general feeling of uptightness.

Along with the physical sensations of the body preparing to act, other subtler feelings can arise. I call them subtler because they may have no counterpart in the physical body (or very little trace of one), but they feel as if they are there. For example, I may say I feel heaviness in my heart. There may not be anything actually happening in that area — no physical weight actually pulling downward — but the sensation is still there. With fear, there may be a sense of wanting to pull back. With desire, a feeling of leaning forward and reaching out. With sadness, a sense of emptiness, perhaps. These are feelings with many of the qualities of an actual bodily sensation, but on a subtler level.

All emotions involve bodily feelings of some kind — physical or subtle. It is no accident, therefore, that we use the word *feeling* both for sensations in the body and for emotions.

But emotions are more than feelings; almost always, some story accompanies them. By story, I mean something we are telling ourselves about what has happened or might happen. If you are angry with someone, you might have a story about how they upset your plans or otherwise got in your way.

Similarly, with fear: you might tell yourself that if you don't negotiate your office politics more skillfully you could soon be out of a job. You then imagine being unable to pay the bills, losing your home, ending up on the street, and so forth.

The story doesn't have to be negative. If you're feeling romantically attracted to someone, you may tell yourself how perfect this person is: they are good-looking, intelligent, and funny; they meet your needs, and will make everything rosy and fine.

There's seldom an emotion without a story behind it. Try to feel angry, sad, jealous, embarrassed, excited, awed, or any other emotion without thinking about the past or future — that is, without telling yourself a story.

You can't. Without the story it doesn't exist.

An emotion has one foot in the primary reality of our present experience — the feeling, physical or subtle — and the other foot in the secondary reality of our imagination, the story we tell ourselves. The two are intertwined in a single experience we call an emotion. It's like having a ball of yarn composed of red and white threads. From a distance the ball would look pink, but on closer examination we'd see it's made up of two different colors.

These two aspects of an emotion — the felt sensation

and the mental story — can feed back on each other, making the emotion more intense and sustaining it far longer than necessary. Suppose, for example, you are having angry thoughts about someone you believe has got in your way. The brain doesn't distinguish between an experience stemming from the physical world and one created in the imagination. It gets ready to attack, leading to associated bodily sensations. These feelings may reinforce the story we've been telling ourselves. Going over it again may then trigger more feelings. And so on. The two reinforce each other, perpetuating an emotion long after it was an appropriate response.

Because emotions bridge both our primary and secondary realities, they have a particularly strong hold on us, which makes letting go of them so challenging. You cannot run away from an emotion. Retreat into the mind; the story is still there. Come back to your present experience; the feelings are still there. So what is the key to letting them go?

LETTING GO *of* FEELINGS

WE ALL HAVE UNCOMFORTABLE EMOTIONS from time to time. And, as with physical discomfort, our first reaction may be to avoid feeling them fully. Why should we feel something unpleasant when what we want is the opposite?

We fear, consciously or otherwise, that if we really got in touch with our anger, we might explode in rage at our boss or partner, starting a chain of events we may well regret. We might avoid feeling a particular sadness, afraid of bursting out sobbing in public. We might not admit to feeling depressed, concerned about what others might think of us. Or we might push difficult feelings to the edges of the mind, where they cannot have much influence; take drugs in order to numb or obscure them; immerse ourselves in other activities to keep the feelings at bay; or, as is often the case, not even acknowledge they are there.

So the first step in letting go of feelings is to let them in.

A few years ago, a person walked into my meditation group by accident; he was looking for a different class but had the wrong date. Nevertheless, he decided to stay, and during the course of the evening revealed how burdened he was by grief, having lost a close family member a few months earlier. Try as he might, he had not been able to overcome it. I suggested that instead of trying to get rid of the grief, he open to it, noticing any bodily sensations associated with it.

In the next meditation, he noticed various feelings — heaviness in the chest, a tight ball in the belly, tearful sensations in the eyes — and allowed them to come into his awareness just as they were. He let them in and let them be. As he did, he felt a growing sense of relief. At the end of the meditation, he reported that the burden had lifted and that he felt much more at ease. And he looked it, too.

In my own life, I've applied this principle when I've felt low for no apparent reason. The feeling would usually last a couple days, and then be gone. But as long as it was there, I found myself resisting it. Feeling low seemed like wasted time. I wanted to be free of it, return to normal, and get on with things.

On one such occasion, I was in my cottage staring out the window at the forest, feeling bad that I was not getting any writing done. For some reason — an intuition, perhaps — I decided to stop resisting the experience and instead became curious about how it actually felt. As I explored the various feelings, I noticed a general sluggishness; my head felt heavy, my mind felt dull. As I opened to them more, I realized what I really wanted was simply to do nothing.

So instead of attempting to change how I was feeling, I decided to do exactly what I felt like doing. In this case, it meant continuing to look out the window, doing nothing. But now I felt OK about it. A couple of hours later, I was my normal self again. I had stopped resisting the discomfort, let it in, given it the attention it needed, and by following its calling, allowed the feelings to unwind.

Sometimes we don't quite know *what* we're feeling; there's just a sense of unease. In these cases, it can be helpful to pause and listen to the body. To allow in whatever feelings may be there, physical or subtle. As we do, we may well find emotions we weren't previously aware of begin to reveal themselves.

At other times, we may be so caught up in an emotional reaction that it can hide what we're truly feeling. That might sound paradoxical because an emotion *is* partly a feeling. I can probably best explain what I mean with an example.

In a recent meeting, I was growing frustrated that some people were straying off topic into personal issues that I thought were a distraction. So I decided to express my feelings. As I talked about my frustration, I noticed some shakiness and a quivering in the chest. Afterward, I realized that what I was really feeling in that moment was anxiety about interrupting the group. The feeling of frustration had the label of an emotion, so I believed that was what I was feeling. But it wasn't. It had become another story about the past. I was so busy explaining what I *had* been feeling that I wasn't fully aware of my true feeling in the present moment — namely, my nervousness about speaking up.

LETTING GO *of* STORY

THE OTHER SIDE OF LETTING GO of emotions is letting go of the story behind them. Again, the first step is to let the story in, to become conscious of what we're telling ourself. This is not always as easy as it sounds. We often assume that our view of events is the truth rather than our interpretation of them.

A good starting point is to pause and explore whether what you believe to be true really is so. Open to the possibility that it may be just a set of assumptions you have made. See if you can step back, question your interpretations, and be open to seeing alternatives.

If you are angry, for example, you might ask, *What am I telling myself that makes this person wrong? How, in my opinion, should they have behaved? How do I judge them for having acted that way?*

I also find it helpful to ask whether I would accuse myself of this. How often, when someone is angry with us, do we feel their anger is unjustified! If only they understood us better and why we behaved as we did, they wouldn't be so angry.

So try putting yourself in the other person's shoes, and consider what might have led them to behave this way. How might they have been seeing you? Did they have other things on their mind? What in their past might have led them to this?

The more we can inhabit another person's point of view, the more we can understand their behavior. If we understood them completely, we'd realize they were behaving exactly as they "should" have — given their situation and everything that came before. Our belief that they should not have behaved this way is another part of our story.

Holding on to our stories only serves to create more suffering and discontent. I was recently visiting a neighbor when a friend came by. Almost the first words out of the friend's mouth were, "I still can't forgive him for what he did." She was clearly still aggrieved and upset, even though the event in question had happened six months earlier. She was holding on to a story about what had happened, and that story still triggered bad feelings — which only reinforced her story. My neighbor simply said to her, "Oh, I'm sorry for you," meaning I'm sorry you're still not over it, "that can't be nice."

When we continue holding on to a grievance long after the event, the only person we hurt is ourself. As the Buddha is purported to have said, holding a grievance is like taking poison and hoping the other person dies.

If you find yourself doing this, the first step in letting go is to become aware of the suffering you're creating for yourself. If you pick up a hot coal, you will let go of it as soon as you feel the pain. Similarly, with holding on to some judgment or grievance, the more you can become aware of the price you pay for holding on — the emotional pain, tension, disturbing thoughts — the more motivated you will be to dig deeper, to see what is going on inside and how you might let go.

Emotions often have more to do with our past than our present. A friend not giving us the attention we feel is our due or criticizing our appearance can touch on painful experiences from earlier in life and trigger reactions out of all proportion to present circumstances. Maybe we felt ignored as a child or had parents who were overly concerned about how we appeared in public. Our automatic reaction might be to storm off in a huff or to retaliate with a criticism of our own. Alternatively, we may act out with something apparently unrelated, such as swearing at the dog or indulging in comfort food.

When you notice unwarranted reactions like these, pause, take a breath, and notice what you're feeling — at this stage, not the story so much as what is going on in your body. Notice where it is tight, feel any unease or discomfort, and observe any impulse to act out. If you can allow these feelings to be there as they are, you may find they begin to soften and not dominate so much.

Then, when they have subsided a little, look at any story you may be telling yourself. Maybe there's some truth to it, but how much have you added? Have any events in your past led you to respond this way? Maybe there are issues you need to explore in order to find some resolution or healing.

Perhaps some childhood trauma lies behind your reaction. The more you understand what is going on, the less likely old wounds will trigger you in the future.

Emotions are impulses to "move out" in some way; they want some form of expression. So with a strong emotion such as anger or rage, it can be helpful to let it out. But rather than venting on a fellow human being, you might take it out on a pillow or a punching bag. Or, a less violent option, you might express to others what you're thinking and feeling, in a safe context — talking to a good friend or a therapist, perhaps — allowing the thoughts and feelings to be there without embarrassment or fear of judgment.

Even then, we might hold something back, fearing others might judge us. Or possibly because we wish to keep part of our life private. In such cases, writing to ourselves about what we are feeling can be a good way to vent our emotions. Simply write down whatever comes (four-letter words and all), without any judgment. Let it all in. Afterward you can tear it up or even burn it if you wish. It's expressing it to yourself that is important.

NOT RESISTING RESISTANCE

AT TIMES WE MAY RESIST experiencing our feelings. We may sense some discomfort percolating beneath the surface but not know exactly what it is or what might happen if we allowed ourselves to fully experience it. How might it feel? Will it overwhelm us? Will we be able to control ourselves once we open the gates?

When we resist a feeling, two things are present: the feeling being resisted and the resistance itself. In such situations, we tend to focus on letting go of the feeling — being free of it is, after all, what we want. But it can be more helpful to first turn our attention to the resistance. That is what is keeping our emotions stuck, preventing us from fully experiencing them. So paying attention to the feeling of resistance is the best place to start.

As before, letting go of resistance means first letting it in, recognizing how it feels to resist. Since the experience of resisting can be very subtle and not easily noticed, I find it useful to simply pause and ask, *Is there any sense of resistance I'm not noticing?* And then gently wait.

Some feelings may then become apparent — perhaps a faint mental tension, a sense of being blocked, or a tightening in the chest or belly. As I let in more of how it feels to resist and let it be, without trying to change it or get rid of it, the resistance often begins to soften and dissolve. Sometimes it simply fades away.

Then, with less resistance, I can be more open to whatever feeling I had been avoiding.

The key to this approach is to include any resistance as part of the present moment. Then, instead of your experience being divided in two — the actual experience in the moment and your resistance to it — the feeling of resistance is now included as part of what is.

THE MATERIALIST MINDSET

HUMANKIND'S EXCEPTIONAL CAPACITY for innovation is a two-edged sword. On the one hand, our ability to learn from the past, imagine new possibilities, make choices, plan changes, and invent tools and technologies to implement them has transformed our world. Look around: just about everything you see, apart from other living beings and the land we inhabit, is the product of human creativity and ingenuity. Behind all this lies the motivation to reduce pain and suffering, live longer and healthier lives, increase comfort and safety, and ultimately feel more at peace. (It may not always work out that way, but that's another story.)

We have been so successful at changing the world, we've come to believe that this is the answer to all our problems. If we're not at peace, we must *do* something about it. We need to rearrange our world, obtain some object, have some new experience, or conversely, avoid some circumstance that might cause distress. We assume that if we could just get our world to be the way we want it, we'd finally be happy. This is the materialist mindset that rules our culture and runs most of our lives.

As children, we learn from the example of our elders that it is important to be in control of things, that material possessions offer security. As we grow up, much of our education focuses on knowing the ways of the world in order to better manage our affairs and thus find contentment and fulfillment. As adults, the daily deluge of television, radio, news, social media, and advertisements reinforces the belief that happiness comes from what we have or do.

Somewhere deep inside, most of us recognize this isn't always true; whether or not we're content can depend as much on how we see things as on how things actually are. We all know people who can remain cheerful when everything seems to be going wrong, who are not upset at having to wait in line, even in the rain. And we hear of more unusual examples — those who have maintained an inner equanimity despite the ravages of war or major health challenges. But because our cultural conditioning is so strong, this inner knowing rarely comes to the surface.

We remain caught in a vicious circle. If we assume that inner contentment comes from what we have or do, that is the message we teach each other. If we see somebody suffering, we will probably suggest ways to change things, hoping it will make the person feel better. When we want to persuade someone to do something, we tell them how much happier they will be.

In the short term, it may appear to work. When we get what we want, we might well feel some pleasure, satisfaction, or contentment. But any happiness we find doesn't last. As soon as one high wears off we go in search of another fix — food, music, driving, debating, sports, television, shopping, or some other favored source of happiness.

When these fail to bring lasting satisfaction, we don't question whether our approach might be mistaken. Instead, we try even harder to have the world give us what we want. We buy more clothes, go to more parties, try to make more money. Or we give up on these and try different things. We take up a new hobby or look for new friends.

We live in what Indian philosophies call samsara, meaning "wandering on endlessly." We wander on endlessly, looking for fulfillment in a world that provides only temporary respites from suffering — passing pleasures followed by more wandering on in search of that ever-elusive goal.

The net result is a semipermanent state of discontent, most of which is self-created.

CREATING DISCONTENT

WHEN ALL IS OK IN OUR WORLD, we feel OK inside, at ease and content. This is the mind in its natural, unperturbed state. When, on the other hand, something is amiss, we feel discontent — a feeling that motivates us to rectify whatever is wrong and so return to feeling OK.

If we're still unhappy, even though there are no immediate needs or threats, the discontent is most likely self-created. We might be dwelling on something from the past we're not happy about; feeling dissatisfied with our present experience; or, more likely, given our basic goal of survival, worrying about what might or might not happen in the future.

We don't realize we'd be happier if we didn't worry so much. Instead, we think the cause of our discontent lies in the world around us and thus seek to feel better in the way we know best — the way our culture has conditioned us to respond — by *doing* something about it.

The advertising industry in particular reinforces this approach, promoting discontent in the present with promises of greater happiness in the future. The underlying message of any advertisement — whether it's for a smartphone, a new car, a vacation package, gourmet food, or fashionable clothing — is that you lack something. You cannot be content as you are. Buy whatever they are selling, and you will feel better.

On the surface, it may seem to work; we make the purchase and, for a while, we do feel better. We think the item we bought has made us happy. But when we examine the process more closely, we find something very different going on.

Discontent arises because we imagine some lack or unfilled need. We assume we can't be happy until we get what is missing. Then, when we do get whatever it is we desire, that particular discontent has gone. We feel better. But it is not getting the object of our desire that made us happy. We feel better because we're no longer creating the discontent that came from *not* having it.

This is readily apparent when we buy something on the internet. The moment we start feeling good about our purchase is the moment we hit the Buy button. It may be several days before we receive what we've bought and begin to enjoy its benefits, but the discontent ends when we make the decision to buy. We're no longer feeling that particular lack, no longer creating that particular discontent.

There is, however, one respect in which the ads are right. We do lack something. But it is not some product, experience, or opportunity. We lack the peace and contentment of natural mind. And that is missing not because it isn't available but because it has been replaced by self-created discontent. A mind that is worried cannot, almost by definition, be a mind that is at peace.

This is the sad truth about human beings: *worrying whether or not we will be at peace in the future prevents us from feeling at peace in the present.*

Some people spend their whole lives this way, never giving themselves the chance to be at peace — until, finally, they can worry no more, and we inscribe Rest in Peace on their tombstones.

But we don't have to wait until we die to rest in peace. At any moment, we can choose to pause our thinking. To cease creating that particular discontent, and relax back into the peace of natural mind.

THE ROOT *of* SUFFERING

THE BUILDING WHERE I used to run a meditation group was on the same street as a fire station. One could almost guarantee that sometime during the meeting a fire engine would come rushing past, sirens wailing. Not surprisingly, people would complain afterward: "How can I meditate with that noise?"

How often have we felt something similar? There's a common assumption that the mind can become quiet only if the world around us is quiet. We imagine the ideal meditation setting to be somewhere far from the madding crowd — a retreat deep in a forest, a peaceful chapel, or perhaps the quiet of one's own bedroom. It is much harder for the mind to settle down in a noisy environment.

Or is it?

I suggested that the next time a fire engine came blaring by, they look within and explore why it was so disturbing. After the next meditation, a woman reported how the noise no longer seemed a problem. It was there, but it didn't disturb her. The disturbance, she realized, came not from the sound itself but from her wishing it weren't there.

This was the essence of Buddha's realization 2,500 years ago. We all experience what he called dukkha, conventionally translated as "suffering." But in Pali, the language of Buddha's time, *dukkha* is the negation of the word *sukha*, meaning "at ease." So *dukkha* might be better translated as "not-at-ease," "discontent," or "unsatisfactoriness" (the term used by some contemporary Buddhist scholars).

Interpreting suffering more generally as discontent casts a gentler light on the notion that "life is suffering." Discontent is an experience we all know. And just as the Buddha sought to be free from suffering, we'd all like to be free from unnecessary discontent.

The root meanings of these words add further insight. *Sukha* stems from *su* (good) and *kha* (hole) and referred to a good axle hole in the wheel of a cart. The wheel was a technological boon of the time, and whether or not it ran smoothly around its axle would have been a primary concern for both efficiency and comfort. Conversely, the root of dukkha is *du* (bad) and *kha* (hole). There is resistance to the smooth running of the wheel, leading to friction and discomfort.

And so it is with the mind. When we let go of resistance, "go with the flow," and accept things as they are, we feel at ease — sukha. This is our natural state of mind, content and relaxed. Dukkha, suffering, arises when we resist our experience. Our natural state of ease is replaced by self-created discontent.

Thus, as Buddha and numerous teachers have pointed

out, we can return to a more peaceful state of mind by letting go of our attachments to how things should be and accepting our experience as it is. Not wishing for something different.

Hearing this, people often ask, Does this mean I should accept injustice and cruelty, the homeless sleeping on the streets, or the recalcitrant attitude of my partner? Of course not. There are numerous situations we should not tolerate, and each of us, in our own way, will be called to do what we can to improve the world.

"Accepting our experience as it is" means just that, accepting our experience as it is, in the moment. If you feel frustrated, angry, or indignant, accept the feeling. Don't resist it or wish it weren't there. Our present experience is as it is. Resistance is futile.

FALLING *from* GRACE

WE DID NOT FALL FROM GRACE at some past point in time. We fall from grace every day — repeatedly falling from the grace of the present moment into the world of time.

The common assumption that happiness comes from what we have or do leads to near-incessant mental chatter telling us what is going on, what we should think, and how we should respond. We might look back to the past. *What went wrong? What could I have done better?* Or we might reminisce about the good times we've had, wondering how we might recapture that happiness. And we worry about the future: *Will it be the way we think it should be for us to be happy? What do we need? How can we get it?*

I am not suggesting that thinking isn't valuable. It has its time and place and has been a critical factor in the evolution of human culture. It helped make us what we are, allowed us to make choices about the future and create a better world for ourselves. But it is both a blessing and a curse. All this thinking takes us out of the present moment. We fall from the grace of now.

It also veils the peace of mind that comes from simply being. Not realizing that much of our discontent is self-created, we seek to ease it by doing something about it. We move from one task to another, ticking off items on our never-ending to-do list, seldom pausing for a moment to smell the roses. Again we fall from grace — from human beings into human doings.

If this were just a sad reflection on the human condition, it would be tragedy enough. However, our striving to find happiness through what we have or do, amplified by our prodigious technological powers, has dangerous repercussions on our world. We are gobbling up the planet's resources at an alarming rate, at the same time discharging more and more waste into our environment. We now face a future that seems to promise not more happiness and joy but increased pain and suffering.

Where did we go wrong? The root cause, as numerous wise ones have pointed out, is that we're looking for happiness and joy in the wrong place.

A popular Sufi tale tells of the wise fool Nasruddin outside his house one night, kneeling on the ground under a streetlamp, looking for his key. A neighbor joins in, scrabbling around in the dirt. After a while he asks, "Where exactly did you lose it?" "In my house," comes the reply. "Well," asks the neighbor, being as tactful as possible, "why are you looking for it out here?" "Because," replies the wise fool, "there's more light out here."

We may laugh at his apparent foolishness, but we can be equally foolish in our search for happiness. We look for it in the world around us because that is the world we know best. We know how to change it, how to gather possessions, how to make people and things behave the way we want. We know much less about our minds; they seem dark and mysterious. And so we keep chasing things and experiences in the external world, not realizing the key to feeling better lies within.

Parallel sentiments can be found in just about every religion. In Christianity, phrases such as "Sinners repent, for the Kingdom of Heaven is at hand" can be interpreted as an admonishment to be sorry for your sins because the day of judgment is coming. But if we look back to the earlier Greek texts, we find another, more everyday interpretation.

The Greek word translated as "sin" is *amartano*. This, as Maurice Nicholl pointed out in his book *The Mark*, is a term in archery meaning to have missed the mark, to have missed the bull's-eye. The bull's-eye we seek is a better state of mind — happiness, contentment, ease, inner peace. However, believing this state comes from what we have or do, we aim in the wrong direction — at things and experiences in the world — and by so doing, we "miss the mark."

The Greek word translated as "repentance" is *metanoia*, meaning "a change of mind." Thus, the phrase can also be translated as "If you have missed the target, and not found happiness in the world, change your mind — for what you seek is right here, within you."

Numerous other spiritual teachers have affirmed that we don't need to do anything or go anywhere to find inner peace. The mind in its natural, unsullied state is already at peace. We simply need to let go of our attachments to how things should be; accept our experience, as it is, without resistance or judgment; and so return to natural mind — to our natural state of grace.

There we find the peace of mind we've been seeking all along. A peace that is not at the mercy of events or the vacillations of the thinking mind. A peace we can return to again and again.

EFFORTLESS MEDITATION

THERE ARE MANY TYPES OF MEDITATION. Some focus attention on the breath, a mantra, an inner light, the heart, or perhaps some deity. Others focus on an intention, a prayer, a future outcome, or some spiritual aphorism. And their goals vary, too. They might aim to help us discover our true nature, transcend the ego, attain a higher state of consciousness, know God, receive guidance or healing, or become enlightened — the list goes on and on.

The meditation practices I am most interested in are those that allow the thinking mind to relax and settle down. The key is allowing it to happen. Instead of trying to focus your attention, let it relax. Let go of any expectation of what should or should not happen.

Simply notice your experience in the moment — the sensations in the body, the flowing of the breath, the sounds you hear. Allowing them to be there, just as they are. Not wanting some other experience; not trying to get somewhere else. This is the essence of letting go — simply letting in your experience, whatever it is, and letting it be.

What about thoughts? People frequently complain that they can't stop thoughts from coming in as they meditate. Having thoughts pass through our mind is natural and unavoidable. Ask experienced meditators if they still have thoughts when they sit, and they'll answer yes. The key is in how we respond to them.

At first you don't notice you're caught in a thought. Your attention gets absorbed in some idea. Maybe it is interesting or feels important. Or, as often happens, it might just arise habitually, a repeat of some idea you've had many times before. After a while, the thought runs out of steam. At that moment, you have become present again — present to the fact that you've been thinking.

Then, instead of continuing with the thought, as you might in everyday life, simply choose not to follow it any further. With the attention no longer absorbed in the thought, the present reveals itself again. You notice the experience of sitting there, the sensations, the breath, the feelings, the sounds around you.

But don't then try to stay present. That's very hard to do. Thoughts will soon arise again. The practice is not one of *staying present* so much as it is learning to *return to the present* — easily, and without effort.

The process is sometimes likened to teaching a puppy to sit. You hold its rear down and say, "Sit." But you don't hold its rear there. You let go, and soon the puppy scampers off. You show it again. And again. Gradually it learns and remains sitting for longer and longer.

It's the same with the mind. We bring our attention back to the present; we sit in the here and now. When the attention wanders off, we gently return it to the present. Gradually, the ease and quietness of natural mind become more familiar — and more attractive — and we find we can settle down more and more easily.

Meditation is, however, more than just enjoying the ease of a quiet mind and then returning to the world with greater calm and composure, lovely as that may be; rather, it is practicing a skill that can serve us in daily life. In training for a sport, we may spend time refining our golf swing or tennis backhand so we can go out on the course or court and put our training into practice. Similarly, with meditation, we refine the skill of letting go, so that when we return to every-day life, we can put it into practice. At any moment we can choose not to follow the current thought, to let go, and to relax back into the ease of a quieter mind.

Moreover, the value of meditation goes beyond how it may help us in daily life. Resting in the stillness, we become more aware of our true self. And the more familiar we become with this essential quality of our being, the freer we are to let go of egoic thinking. And *that's* a good thing for all concerned.

SAVORING *the* MOMENT

Now is the only moment we will ever know. Our memories of the past are experiences in the present. So are our thoughts about the future. So when we talk about not being present, we mean our attention is not on the present moment. It is focused on thoughts about the past or future.

We can be present in three ways. First, we can live for today, not worrying about yesterday or about what tomorrow may bring. This attitude has its value. It can help us take life as it comes and not get so troubled by unnecessary fears and concerns. But it does not necessarily lead to fuller awareness of the present moment itself. We may still be as caught up in thoughts as before, even if they are thoughts about today rather than about yesterday or tomorrow.

A second way, common to many meditation practices, is being aware of our current experience. Whereas most of our thoughts are about the past or the future, our sensory experience is always "now." This is why basic meditation techniques often focus the attention on the body — the heartbeat, the breath, or some other sensation. The feelings in the body are always in the present.

And there is a third way of being present that can develop from this: *being present to how it is to be present* — not so much noticing your experience of the moment but noticing how it feels to be in the moment.

You may have a sense of ease, of relief and relaxation, of deeper contentment, inner peace, joy. Perhaps a sense of openness or spaciousness. Or a gentle delight in the mind being quiet, an appreciation of the inner stillness. However it feels, allow yourself to savor it. To soak in it, as you might soak in a warm bath.

Savoring how it actually feels to be present motivates us to return here more often. As we do, the familiar, delightful feeling of being here now becomes a beacon drawing us home.

JUST PAUSE

Pause.

Just pause. Nothing else.

And notice your experience. Notice what is there. In this moment.

There will be various perceptions — sights, sounds, smells. Bodily sensations of one kind or another. Perhaps some feelings or a general mood. And most likely, along with these, some thoughts. Maybe some strong ones dominating your attention. Or some fainter ones in the background — some commentary, perhaps, about what is going on or maybe some habitual concern.

When you notice you are thinking, choose to pause it. Just for a moment.

In choosing to pause, you're not choosing to do something else but to simply stop following the thought. To withdraw your interest from it.

And then let the attention relax.

You may notice a sense of ease, a feeling of relief,

perhaps, a gentle sense of happiness or joy, a sense of spaciousness and clarity, a lightness of being, or some similar quality.

If so, savor it. Enjoy how it feels to pause for a moment.

At times you may notice subtler levels of thinking in the background — reflections on what you're noticing, perhaps, or other thoughts that have quietly wandered in.

Choose not to follow them either. Let them go for now.

Notice what it's like to be free of them. Not caught up in doing.

Later, whenever it occurs to you, pause again.

And again …

But don't let the practice of pausing become routine, as in looking for similar experiences, responding in the same way. Don't let it become a ritual that you *do*. For then the practice will lose its value and power.

Make each pause a fresh inquiry into the moment. Be curious about what it feels like — as if it were the first time.

Which it is. The first — and only — time you will savor *this* moment.

THE PARABLE *of the* ROPE

WE ARE LIKE SOMEONE HOLDING ON TO A ROPE.

He holds on for dear life, knowing that if he lets go he will surely fall. His parents, his teachers, and many others have told him this is so. And as he looks around, he sees everyone else holding on tightly. Nothing would induce him to let go.

Along comes a wise person. She knows that holding on doesn't help, that any security it offers is illusory and only keeps us where we are. So she looks for a way to dispel his illusions and set him free.

She talks of a deeper joy, of true happiness, and inner peace. She tells him he can taste these if he will release one finger from the rope.

One finger, thinks the man, *that's not too much to risk for a taste of bliss.* So he agrees to this first initiation.

And he does indeed taste more joy, happiness, and inner peace.

But not enough to bring lasting fulfillment.

"Even more joy and happiness can be yours," she says, "if you will just release a second finger."

This, he tells himself, *is going to be more difficult. Will I be safe? Do I have the courage?*

He hesitates, then, flexing a finger, feels how it would be to let go a little more ... and takes the risk.

He is relieved to find he does not fall. Instead he discovers a greater happiness and peace of mind.

But could more be possible?

"Trust me," she says. "Have I failed you so far? I know your fears, I know what your mind is telling you — that this is crazy, that it goes against everything you have ever learned — but please, trust me. I promise you will be safe and will know even greater peace and contentment."

Do I really want inner peace so much, he wonders, *that I'm prepared to risk all I've held dear? In principle, yes; but can I be sure I won't fall?*

With a little coaxing, he begins to look at his fears, consider their origin, and explore what he really wants. Slowly, he feels his third finger soften and relax. He knows he can do it. He knows he must do it. It is only a matter of time before he releases this finger, too.

And as he does, an even greater sense of ease flows through him.

He is now hanging by one finger. Reason tells him he should have fallen a finger or two ago, but he hasn't. *Is there something wrong with holding on?* he asks himself. *Have I been mistaken all along?*

"This one is up to you," she says. "I can help you no further. Just remember that all your fears are groundless."

Trusting his own quiet inner voice, he gradually releases the last finger.

And nothing happens.

He stays exactly where he is.

Then he realizes why. All along, he has been standing on the ground.

REDISCOVERING
the TIMELESS WISDOM

MOST SPIRITUAL TRADITIONS began with a person having some transforming mystical experience, a profound revelation or inner awakening. It may have come through dedicated spiritual practice, deep devotion, or facing a hard challenge, or sometimes it came unbidden, out of the blue — a timeless moment in which personal dramas paled in the light of a deep inner peace and serenity. However it came, it usually led to a delightful joy in being alive, an unconditional love for all beings, and the dissolution of a personal self.

Experiencing such profound transformations has led many to want to share their discoveries and help others have their own awakening. But those who heard their teachings may have misunderstood some parts, forgotten others, and perhaps added interpretations of their own. Much like the party game Telephone, in which a message whispered around a room can end up nothing like the original, as the teachings were passed from one person to another, from one culture to another, and were translated from one language to another, they gradually became less and less like the original. The timeless wisdom became clothed in the beliefs and values of the society in which it found itself, resulting in a diversity of faiths whose common essence is often hard to detect.

Today, however, we are in the midst of a spiritual renaissance that differs significantly from those of the past. We are no longer limited to the faith of our own culture; we have access to many traditions, from the dawn of recorded history to the present day. Moreover, the insights of contemporary teachers from around the world are readily available in books, audio recordings, and videos, as well as on the internet. None of this was possible before.

Whereas previous spiritual revivals were usually led by a single teacher, there are today many experiencing and expounding the perennial philosophy. Some may be more visible than others, and some may have clearer realizations than others, but all contribute to a growing rediscovery of the timeless wisdom.

Instead of the truth becoming progressively diluted and veiled as it is passed on, today our discoveries are reinforcing one another. We are seeing through the differences of the world's faiths, past their various cultural trappings and interpretations, to what lies at their heart.

As we strip away layers of accumulated obscurity, the core message not only becomes increasingly clear, it gets simpler and simpler. And the path becomes easier and easier.

There is a growing recognition that inner awakening does not need studious reading of spiritual texts, years of meditation practice, or deep devotion to a teacher but only the willingness to engage in an honest investigation into our own being. Not an intellectual investigation, but a personal inquiry into who and what we truly are.

THERE'S NO SUCH THING *as* EGO

THERE'S NO SUCH THING AS EGO. That doesn't mean you and I don't get caught up in egocentric thinking and behavior, but we are mistaken when we regard the ego as some separate self, some "thing" in the mind.

When I observe my own experience, I notice an unchanging sense of "I-ness" that has been there all my life. It's that feeling of being me and is the same feeling I had yesterday, a year ago, and when I was ten years old. My thoughts, emotions, character, personality, desires, needs, beliefs, and preferences may have changed considerably over the years, but this sense of "I" has not.

Along with this sense of self, I might find various thoughts about what I want, what would make me happy, or what would give me more control over my world — what we might label "egocentric" thoughts. I might, at times, feel fearful or judgmental. I might think that if I could just have things be a particular way, I would be happy. But I don't find a distinct self, or ego — an entity that is having these thoughts.

What we call the ego is not some part of me; it is a mode of thinking, a process rather than a thing, a verb rather than a noun. We could say: *I am ego-ing.*

The difference is subtle but very important. If we see ego as some distinct self, it is easy to fall into the belief — common in many spiritual circles — that we must get rid of our ego, transcend it, or overcome it in some way. But seeing ego as a mode of thinking we get caught in leads to a very different approach. Letting go of ego becomes letting go of a thought system. And that can be an ongoing practice rather than a far-off goal.

LETTING GO *of* EGO

THE EGO WE SHOULD LET GO OF is not what psychologists call a "healthy ego," a sense of self-worth important for full psychological development that helps us form meaningful relationships and cope with the challenges of life, but the self-centered mode of thinking that assumes happiness depends on what we have or do, leading us to use the world for our own ends.

There are, needless to say, times when this approach is important. If our well-being or safety is at risk, it's completely natural to make our personal welfare a priority. Egoic thinking, as such, is not an enemy. It is an *ally*, there to help us survive.

The downside arises when this mode of thinking is activated more than necessary. It hijacks our attention, creating discontent when none is needed, triggering emotions we'd be better off without, obsessing over getting what we think will make us happy, solving problems that don't yet exist and may never come to pass — all of which overshadows our experience of the present moment, veiling the peace and contentment of the natural, unperturbed mind.

Seeing ego as a way of thinking we get caught in — we could call it ego-mind — rather than some *thing* we need to control or eliminate makes the task of freeing ourselves from its grip much easier. When we notice egoic thoughts arising, we can simply choose not to follow them.

Yet, as most of us can testify, it is seldom that easy.

For a start, the ego-mind can be active so much of the time it seems normal. If you wear rose-tinted spectacles all the time, you forget what the world looks like without them. Similarly with the ego-mind: its view of reality can easily become the "truth." If, for example, you hold a certain mindset about your national leader, it can become the reality through which you interpret his or her actions, making it very challenging for someone to make you change your mind.

In addition, egoic thinking wants to be taken seriously. It has a job to do: keeping us safe. If our well-being is truly at stake, it needs us to follow its planned course of action. The fact that the same response can be triggered by some imagined threat is irrelevant. Once triggered, it is up and running, demanding we follow its bidding.

This insistence can be a clue to spotting when we are caught in egoic thinking. When the voice in your head seems particularly strong, persuading you of the right thing to do and not wanting to hear alternatives, it might be time to pause and consider whether ego-mind might be in full swing. Step back for a moment, notice what the voice is saying, and consider how true that is.

Another way of recognizing egoic thinking is the background mental tension that can accompany it. Much of the time, this tension is so faint we don't notice it. But we may occasionally sense it as a slight tightening or constriction in the mind. It comes from two sources. First, focusing our attention on some idea or issue that seems important can take a small unconscious effort, resulting in a slight mental tension. Second, most of our egoic thoughts have an element of discontent, contributing further to the tension.

This faint mental tension is the hallmark of the ego. So when you notice it, allow your attention to relax, and explore whether you might be caught in some egoic pattern of thought. And if so, inquire whether there might be another way of seeing things.

But be careful: ego-mind is not open to seeing things differently. It thinks it knows what is right and cannot see beyond its own mindset to a radically different point of view. We must get help from a different quarter, from the part of us that remains untouched by the voice of the ego. We need to let in the wisdom of the untainted mind.

PRAYING *to* SELF

WE USUALLY THINK OF PRAYER as an appeal to some higher power. We might pray for someone's healing, for success in some venture, for a better life, or for guidance on some challenging issue. Behind such prayers is the belief that we don't have the power to change things ourselves — if we did, we'd simply get on with the task. So we beseech a higher power to intervene on our behalf.

But what really needs changing? Usually, we want the world to change. We want the circumstances we think will make us happy — or, conversely, we want to avoid those we think will make us suffer. However, when we look more closely at why we aren't happy, we may find that the root of our discontent lies not so much in the situation at hand but in how we perceive it.

If I'm stuck in a traffic jam, for example, I can see it as something that will make me suffer in some way — being late for an appointment, missing some opportunity, or upsetting someone — and begin to feel anxious, frustrated, or impatient. Alternatively, I can see it as an opportunity to relax and take it easy for a few minutes. Same situation, two very different responses. And the difference comes purely from how I see things.

So when I catch myself feeling upset about something, I find it helpful to remember that my annoyance might come from how I am seeing the situation rather than from the situation itself. If that is the case, it makes more sense to ask not for a change in the world but for a change in my perception of it.

And that is what I pray for. I settle into a quiet state and then ask, with an attitude of innocent curiosity, *Could there perhaps be another way of seeing this?* I don't try to answer the question myself; to do so would doubtless activate my ego-mind, which loves to try to work out what to do. I simply pose the question. Let it go. And wait.

Often a new way of seeing dawns on me. It doesn't come as an idea but as an actual shift in perception. I find myself seeing the situation in a new way.

The results of praying like this never cease to impress me. I find my fears and grievances dropping away. In their place is a sense of ease. Whoever or whatever was troubling me, I now see through more loving and compassionate eyes. The beauty of this approach is that I am not praying for intervention in the world but for intervention in my mind. For that's where help is needed most.

Nor am I praying to some external power. I am praying to my own being for guidance — to the unperturbed mind that sees things as they are without the overlay of hopes and fears. It recognizes when I'm caught in egoic ways of thinking and is ever willing to help set me free.

WHO AM I?

WHO ARE YOU? When people first encounter this question, they may respond with answers such as: I am Jill, a woman, an American. I am a Buddhist, a socialist, a vegetarian. I am a mother, a child, a partner. I am a therapist, a teacher, a homemaker. I am smart, funny, caring. The list can go on and on. But is this who you truly are? These are roles you play, things you do, personal characteristics, and abilities you possess. Any of these could change, but the "you" that has these qualities and plays these roles would still be there.

What is this sense of "you" that is always present? That is the intended focus of the question. It points to an ever-present sense of I-ness that has been there all your life, as far back as you can remember. And it never changes.

Some call it the pure self, the true self, or simply the Self, with a capital S to distinguish it from our everyday identities. However, the word *self*, being a noun, can lead us to search for some entity or experience that fits the description of "I." That is a bit like taking a torch into a dark room and looking for the source of the light. All you find are various objects the light shines on, but never the light itself. In the same way, if you go looking for a self, all you will find are various ideas, feelings, and sensations but, however subtle or self-like these experiences might be, they are all experiences you're aware of — not the "I" that is aware of them.

The question is not one to be answered so much as to be held as an inquiry — an invitation to explore what "I" refers to. Not to think about it, but to look into your actual experience and inquire: *What do you mean by "I"? What is the truth here beyond any ideas you have of the self?* Don't look for an answer. Just sit in the inquiry, with an open mind. And the Self will begin to reveal itself to itself.

Another more direct approach is to drop *who* from the question and simply ask, "Am I?" The answer will usually come as a simple, "Yes, I am." Not "I am this or that." Just pure *I am*.

I am is the first-person form of the verb *to be*. It is our direct knowing of being — how being feels to us. Not to be anything or anyone, but just to *be*, to exist. It is a sense of personal presence at the heart of every experience — a presence we call "I."

This "I" is often said to be ineffable, meaning that it cannot be put into words. This is not because we don't have the words to describe it, but because it has no qualities to be described. If it did, they would be qualities that were known — more objects of experience — rather than the subject of them all.

If it has no describable qualities, there is no way to distinguish my sense of "I" from yours. In terms of our personal identities, our needs and values, and how we experience the world, we are very different. I might get some idea of how it is to be you from what you tell me about your various thoughts and feelings, but I can never fully know what it's like to be that particular you.

On the other hand, I do know exactly what that core sense of "I" is like for you. It is the same as it is for me. And for every other person. We all share the same sense of being.

In that, we are all one.

SAT-CHIT-ANANDA

SAT-CHIT-ANANDA IS A COMMON THEME in Indian teachings, usually translated as "truth-consciousness-bliss," or something along those lines. Some interpret it as a state of consciousness to be attained, leading people to look for, or hope for, some exotic new experience. But if we go back to the texts where the term first appears some 2,500 years ago, we find *sat-chit-ananda* to be a description of the Self.

The Sanskrit word *sat* means "true essence" or "that which is and never changes." It is the present participle of the verb *to be*, so it could be literally translated as "being" — again pointing to "I am" as the direct knowing of our own being.

Chit means "consciousness." To be is to be conscious. Not that *I* am conscious, in the sense of an individual called "I" that is conscious or has consciousness. But I *am* consciousness.

Ananda has often been translated as "bliss," which conjures up notions of some ecstatic or euphoric happiness. This translation probably came from early Western translators of

Eastern texts, who had little personal experience of these states, doing the best they could from their own cultural understanding. Now that more of us have tasted the states these teachings were pointing toward, we can appreciate another interpretation of the term.

The Sanskrit word *ananda* stems from *ānanda*. *Nanda* means "contentment" or "satisfaction." The prefix *ā* (the long *a* as in "part" rather than the short *a* as in "pat") is used to denote strong emphasis. So *ānanda* means *great* contentment — the great contentment that comes from returning to our own being.

Resting there, we find a natural ease to which nothing needs be added — or can be added. There are no desires for anything else and no striving to be anywhere — or anyone — else. We may indeed call it bliss, but most often it is a quiet, still bliss rather than the ecstatic happiness we usually associate with the term.

Here we find the ultimate goal of all our desires — that is, a more satisfying, peaceful state of mind — without having to spend time and energy chasing their fulfillment. Buddhists refer to this state as nirvana, the root meaning of which is "to blow out," as in blowing out a candle flame. The flame of desire has been extinguished, not through control or austerity, but through arriving at what we've been seeking all along. There is nothing more to be desired.

People may then ask, If we are resting in such fulfillment, at ease and at peace, with the underlying goal of all our desires satisfied, would we still want to do anything? Yes, there would still be a motivation to act, but it would no longer come from ego-mind, from personal discontent or suffering. It would come from the heart, from compassion for others.

If we saw someone suffer in some way, we'd naturally want to help — either to relieve their suffering in some worldly way or to help them awaken to the cause of suffering. The same would apply to any other creature we saw suffering. We'd want to help. To paraphrase the Buddha, the awakened ones do not rest till they have seen the end of suffering for all beings.

REFRAMING ENLIGHTENMENT

Spiritual enlightenment is often seen as some far-off goal, attained by a few after years of dedicated practice or, on occasion, from some good fortune. It is something we get or achieve, another state of consciousness we are blessed with, supplanting our mundane everyday consciousness. But enlightenment is not some new amazing or ecstatic experience. Nor need it take years of practice. It is simply awakening from the dreamworld of the ego-mind. It is the result of fully letting go.

Our primary reality is the world of our sensory experience: what we see, hear, taste, smell, and feel in the present moment. Along with this is the world of our thoughts, the stories we tell ourselves about what is going on, about what we need and how to achieve it. This is the world of the imagination where we dive into the past and the future, reflecting on our experience, ruminating on possibilities, making choices and plans.

There is nothing wrong with being in the world of imagination. It is valuable to be able to think about our experience, dream of different futures, and plan how to create them. It lies behind so much of what makes us human — our culture, science, technology, art, and philosophy. It is a realm to go to when needed. And then, when we are done, we can return to the primary reality of here and now.

But our imagined worlds are so engrossing, and seem so important, we tend to spend most our time there. Our attention becomes dominated by the stories we tell ourselves, our hopes and fears, our desires and aversions. It is the world of the ego-mind, looking out for our survival, for what will make us safe and secure, meet our needs, and bring us happiness. Such thoughts overshadow our present experience, veiling our true nature. Worse still, they trap us in seeking happiness through what we have or do.

There can, however, come a time when we realize that all our seeking for possessions, fame, fortune, or whatever else we believe will make us happy does not bring lasting satisfaction. All these things serve to perpetuate samsara, that endless wandering on from one temporary gratification to another. This realization is, for many, the first step in waking up.

We may then be drawn to some spiritual teaching that promises a more permanent happiness, independent of the material world. So we start down a path seeking to *get* enlightened. More often than not, the ego-mind kicks in. It thinks this is the answer to our search for happiness. This is what we must find and achieve. We must get enlightened.

We might be tempted to criticize people for pursuing spiritual paths with such egocentric motives. However, as

Indian teachings are wont to point out, it can take a thorn to remove a thorn — that is, it can take the ego-mind to set us out on a journey of awakening that ultimately takes us beyond the ego-mind.

We may try various approaches, and we may well have some remarkable experiences along the way, but sooner or later we recognize that enlightenment is not some new experience, some exalted state in which we will be transformed. It is simply waking from the dream.

This is what mystics of all times and cultures have tasted, some fleetingly, others abiding in its grace. Repeatedly, they attest to the peace, love, and freedom that come with awakening. They attest to the discovery of their true nature. To a sense of the sacred. To the timelessness of the eternal present. To the dissolution of boundaries and oneness with the cosmos.

Some wake up, and that is it. They remain awake. For the vast majority of us, however, we get glimpses — maybe in meditation, perhaps through some intense elation or some other circumstance that results in a profound letting go. But it does not last. It is not long before we find ourselves once again caught in the throes of discontent. And the moment of awakening becomes but a memory.

Yet we have tasted it. And that can be a motivation to return. Each time we do, it becomes more familiar. We are able to recognize more easily when we're stuck in egoic thoughts, and more able to let go.

Indian teachings liken the process to dyeing a cloth. The old vegetable dyes were not that fast and quickly faded. So a cloth was dipped in dye and left out in the sun to fade. Then it was dipped again and left to fade again. Gradually, the color built up until it eventually became permanent.

Similarly, we dip into the ease and freedom of our true nature. It fades some as we engage again in the world. We dip in again. And again, and gradually the freedom grows.

THE PATH *of* NO PATH

SOME SPIRITUAL TEACHERS CLAIM that there is no path to enlightenment. That there is no need for techniques or practices. They say do not meditate; do nothing.

There certainly is a profound truth behind such statements. With awakening comes the realization that, in the words of Lin-chi, one of the founders of Chinese Zen, there is "Nothing to do. Nowhere to go. No one to be."

Enlightenment is not the attainment of some higher state of consciousness or some new extraordinary experience. It is letting go of all that takes us away from the present, from the delight of just being. There is nowhere to get to but here.

If there is nowhere to get to, there is nothing to do. It is our incessant doing that is the problem. When we let go of our attachments to how things should be and return to the joy of our true nature, we find what we've been looking for all along, but we were looking for it in the world rather than in ourselves.

The world remains as it is, and our experience remains

as it is. What changes is our sense of self. We no longer identify as a unique, personal self. There is no longer anyone to be, no persona that needs to express itself or seek recognition and affirmation. We recognize what we really are and always have been: the "I" at the heart of every experience.

From this perspective, there is nowhere to get to. There is no path.

And yet ... many of these same teachers did tread a path. Some spent years investigating the Self. Others may have followed a path of total surrender, a radical deconstruction of experience, or some contemplative practice. My own realizations have come in periods of deep meditation, when my mind was relaxed and still. In those times, it was obvious beyond any doubt that there really is nowhere to get to and nothing to do. And yet, if I had not followed a path that taught me to let go and drop back into this natural state of mind, I would not have appreciated the profound truth of Lin-chi's words.

So from the point of view of the yet-to-be-enlightened mind, there are paths to follow — paths that help us develop the skill of letting go, allowing the thinking mind to settle down; paths that facilitate being here now; paths that help remove the blocks to awareness of the ever-present, unchanging Self. Paths that encourage taking time learning to do nothing.

RETIRE

RETIRE.

No, not at the end of your working life, when you finally retire from earning a living and get to take more time for yourself. Retire now, in everyday life.

Let the mind retire.

Let your attention step back from whatever might be occupying your mind. Become aware of what was already there before the thought caught hold.

Maybe there's an emotion, a feeling, some sensations in the body, your breath, the sounds around you. It doesn't matter what it is. Different experiences become apparent at different times. Just notice whatever is already there but had until now passed unnoticed.

Then retire again. Let the attention step back to become aware of what is there, beneath the sensations and feelings.

Again, there is no right answer. The process itself is what's valuable. Just pause and notice what is there.

And then, retire again.

And again …

BECOMING SOMEONE ELSE

WHY DO WE HAVE THIS SENSE OF BEING an individual self? Where does it come from?

When I try to find this self, I find only various thoughts, feelings, and sensations, all of which come and go. I don't find a permanent self that is thinking the thoughts or feeling the feelings. Just an awareness of them as they arise.

And when I look for an "I" that is aware of them, I again find nothing. Indeed, anything I might identify as my aware self would be another experience of some kind, not the "I" that is aware of the experience.

Yet I still have this very real and persistent sense of being a unique self. It feels like there is a "me" here, living in the body, and the world "out there" that is not me — what Alan Watts dubbed *the skin-encapsulated ego*.

This sense of being in a body has a tangible quality. There's a sense of aliveness to the body, subtle feelings in the skin and muscles, sensations of movement, all contributing to a distinct feeling of inhabiting a body.

Looking around, we see other bodies and assume each

has its own inner self, separate and unique, with its own identity and character.

Believing our own sense of self to be real, and different from other selves, we look for ways to describe and define it. We identify with how we are seen in the world, the roles we play, our social status and profession; with our nationality, our name, our family; with our beliefs, our education, our interests — all the things we initially come up with when asked, "Who are you?" These, and the many other qualities we identify with, can be thought of as the clothes we dress our self in. In this case, however, rather than the emperor having no clothes, we see lots of clothes but we find no emperor underneath.

We also derive a sense of identity from our history, from where we've been and what we've done. We become a character in our own story, on our own hero's journey through the drama of life — navigating the ups and downs, facing challenges and adversity, gathering knowledge and achieving goals, meeting other characters, falling in love with some, fighting others, always traveling on through time into new and uncertain futures.

With an engrossing novel, our attention can become so absorbed in the drama and the characters' adventures, we forget we are the reader of the story. In a similar way, we can be so absorbed in our own dramas, we forget we are that which is aware of the story of our life — along with its hero called "me."

Our experience of thinking strengthens the illusion of an individual self. Many of our thoughts are inner conversations we have with ourselves, commentaries on what is happening, on what we need to do, on how to do it, and so forth. This self-talk appears as a voice in the head — a very familiar voice, one that sounds like us. So we assume this voice *is* "me." We believe we are the thinker of our thoughts rather than that which is aware of them.

In addition, we notice there is consciousness and with it a sense of I-ness. How could we not? It's there at the heart of every experience. We then easily assume that this feeling of I-ness belongs to our personal self. That *it* has consciousness.

But consciousness was there before this self formed. Way back when you were very young and a sense of identity had not yet developed, you were conscious. And when the sense of self dissolves, as can happen in some mystical experiences, you are still conscious, but now you are conscious of there being no personal self.

Everything this self identifies with is arising in consciousness. The feeling of being in a body, the clothes the self dresses up in, the story of its journey through life, the voice in the head: they are all things you are aware of. But you, as awareness, exist independently of any identity as an individual self.

RIPPLES *of* KNOWING

WHAT ARE THOUGHTS MADE OF?

They are not material things; they are not made of atoms or anything physical. Yet our thoughts clearly exist. What, then, is their substance?

Because we don't often consider this question, we don't have any ready words for the stuff mental phenomena are made of. Perhaps the best we can say is they are made from mind-stuff. That in itself doesn't say much, except to emphasize that they are not made of matter-stuff.

Thoughts generally consist of self-talk, images, memories, and such. What is their common element? They all arise in consciousness. So one might say they are made from, or in, consciousness. But what does *consciousness* mean here?

The suffix *-ness* in *consciousness* means "the state or quality of." Happiness is the state of being happy. Softness is the quality of being soft. But neither happiness nor softness exists as independent things. Similarly, *consciousness* means "the state or quality of being conscious." But consciousness does not exist as an independent thing.

The word *conscious* derives from the Latin *conscius* — literally, "with knowing." Thoughts appear with our knowing of them. We could say they appear in our field of knowing — by which I mean the mental space in which all experiences appear and are known.

Thoughts are like waves in the ocean. A wave is just water in motion. It does not exist as an independent entity, separate from the water. We may see the wave as a shape or form, but in essence it is just an activity — an excitation and movement of the water. Similarly, thoughts are an excitation, or stirring, of our field of knowing — they are ripples of knowing.

The same is true of other mental phenomena. If you close your eyes and explore the experience of your body, you will find various sensations — some pressure in places, a warmth here, some tension there perhaps. These experiences, too, are but ripples of knowing.

It works the same way with sound. It is easy to appreciate this when we imagine a piece of music. That clearly is an experience arising in the mind. But there is no essential difference when we hear live music. The brain is taking data relayed to it from the ears, creating from it a representation of the sound, which then appears in the mind as music. The sound we experience is just another ripple of knowing. But it is perceived as coming from an external world beyond the body — the so-called real world.

This world appears all the more real as soon as we open our eyes.

Vision takes us out into the apparent space of an external world that seems to be real and filled with material objects. But however real it might appear, we are forced to accept that the visual experiences themselves are also more ripples of knowing.

This is where it begins to get mind-bending. The colors we experience are just appearances in the mind. The light itself does not have color; it is simply energy with a particular frequency, the color coming from the representation of that frequency in the mind. The same is true of every other quality we experience. We seem to be experiencing the world directly, but in truth all that we experience is a representation of the world out there appearing in our field of knowing.

The fact that we never experience the external world directly doesn't mean we don't know anything about it. But all our knowledge of the world comes from exploring the representation of it in the mind, and from that drawing conclusions about the physical world. This is what science aims to do, to deduce how the world operates. But all we discover — all we know and understand about the world, all our scientific theories and mathematical equations, all our concepts of matter, energy, space, and time, our ideas about quarks, strings, particles, and waves — are but phenomena in the mind. More ripples of knowing.

WHERE AM I?

To the question, *Who* are you? we might answer, The "I am" at the heart of all knowing.

When are you? "Now" is the obvious answer. I am always in the present moment, even though my thoughts may be about the past or the future.

Where are you? "Here" you might say. Where else?

But what do you mean by *here*? You'd probably point to the particular place where your body happens to be. And it's easy to assume this is also where your consciousness is located.

Right now these words may appear a foot or two in front of you. Further in front of you may be a table, and perhaps through a window, some more distant scene; there is the ground beneath you, an awareness of the space behind you. The world seems to be arrayed around you, around the "I" that is aware of it all.

This sense of "I" feels as if it is somewhere in the head. That makes sense in so far as our brains are in our heads. And brains are somehow associated with consciousness. We would find it strange if we felt our self to be somewhere in our knees.

But all is not as it seems. The apparent location of your consciousness doesn't actually have anything to do with the location of your brain. Rather, it depends on the placement of your senses.

Your sense of location in space comes primarily from your eyes and ears, which happen to be located on your head. Thus, the central point of your perception — the point from which you seem to be experiencing the world — is somewhere behind your eyes and between your ears ... somewhere, that is, in the middle of your head. The fact that your brain is also in your head is just a coincidence, as the following thought experiment bears out.

Imagine that your eyes and ears were transplanted to your knees, and that you saw and heard the world from this new vantage point. Where would you now experience your self to be? In your head? Your brain may still be in your head, but it would no longer be the central point of your perception. You would be perceiving the world from a different location and would feel your self to be at the center of this new view — that is, somewhere in your knees!

In short, the impression that your consciousness has a location in space is an illusion. You quite naturally feel yourself to be at the center of your experience — at the center of your perceived world. But your perceived world appears in your consciousness and in that sense is *within* you.

Your consciousness is not someplace in the world; in fact, just the opposite is true. The world as you know it appears in consciousness. And you then mistakenly assume your consciousness to be at the center of this appearance.

FREE WON'T

WHETHER OR NOT WE HAVE FREE WILL in the sense of being free to choose what to do and when to do it, there is another sense in which the will can be free — not *freedom to* so much as *freedom from* — freedom from the ego's will.

The ego-mind looks out for what will keep us safe. Its will is strong, as it needs to be. If our well-being is at stake, it needs to make decisions and be insistent on its course of action. But more often than not, it has been triggered by some imagined need or danger, and its will may no longer be in our best interests.

When we leave ego-mind behind, we find a new kind of freedom. Freedom from the discontent that motivates much of our thinking, freedom from the urge to do something, freedom to rest in the ease and comfort of our natural being.

With this comes the freedom to choose not to choose.

When faced with a decision, rather than letting the thinking mind work out what is best, we can choose to pause our thinking. We can choose not to follow a particular line of thought any further.

The thinking will soon come back, but in that moment we've broken the chain. We've stepped out of conditioned patterns of thought. We are free to start anew. I think of this as *free won't*, as in I won't go there in my mind any longer.

So when you notice you're thinking about something you want but that you know you don't need or might not really be good for you, you can exercise free won't and nip the desire in its bud before the thought flowers into something you then have to resist.

Or if you are focused on planning for some eventuality that in all probability may never happen, choose not to follow the thought any further, and save yourself unnecessary worry and tension.

If you find yourself going over some grievance from the past, choose to let it be, and find peace in the stillness of your own being.

Free won't is true freedom of will. Freedom from the will of ego-mind.

The freedom to choose not to choose. Choosing nothing instead of something.

THE SUPPORT *of* NATURE

CARL JUNG COINED THE WORD *synchronicity* to refer to the remarkable coincidences most of us experience from time to time. They are remarkable in that they usually involve two or sometimes more unconnected events coming together in an unlikely way. These events seem to be more than just coincidences, more than pure chance. They can often seem like miracles, bringing us just what we need at just the right time, opening up new opportunities in our lives or supporting us in some other way.

To give just one example, on a long drive home from a retreat, I decided to leave the main road and explore some country lanes to find a quiet place to take a break. I stopped at a gate to enjoy the view, and a few minutes later one of the retreat leaders walked by. I had wanted to meet him again but had no idea he lived in this part of the country — let alone down this lane.

The Maharishi, with whom I had the good fortune to study in India, explained this as "the support of nature." When he wanted to assess how we were progressing in our practice, he was not so interested in our experiences in meditation itself, such as whether we were aware of the pure Self or tasting higher states of consciousness; he was more interested in whether we had noticed what he called "increased support of nature." By this he meant, did we notice the world supporting our needs and intentions? That is to say, did we notice more synchronicity in our lives?

He reasoned as follows. Much of our thinking stems from egocentric needs and desires. This self-centeredness lies behind many of our problems — from international and environmental problems to social and personal problems. In meditation we transcend ("go beyond") the ego-mind. We are freeing ourselves from its misguided values and thus supporting nature in the most fundamental way. And nature returns the favor by supporting us!

It might sound like magical thinking, but I've noticed that the degree of synchronicity in my life often reflects my state of consciousness. When I meditate regularly, especially when I have been on a meditation retreat, life seems to work out well, with many little coincidences leading me to just what I need at just the right time. It's as if the Universe has my best interests at heart and arranges for their fulfillment in ways I could never have dreamed of.

Conversely, when I'm stressed, not in touch with myself but caught up in worry or in some other way off-center, synchronicities don't flow as abundantly.

Furthermore, synchronicities seem to happen more often when I'm engaged with the world. I can sit alone in a cottage in the middle of a forest, at peace and in touch with myself, yet few synchronicities occur. Significant ones nearly always involve other people in some way. It is as if my interplay with others gives cosmic choreography greater opportunities to reach me.

Although we cannot *make* synchronicities happen — it's in their nature to occur "by coincidence" — we can *encourage* their occurrence. We can support nature by taking time to step back from our egoic thinking and reconnect with our essential being. Then, grounded in our true nature, we can go out and engage fully in the world. We can go out and play — play whatever game or role best fits our intentions and best serves our awakening, and that of others.

And then enjoy, and perhaps marvel at, the way nature responds by supporting *us*.

FORGIVENESS

FORGIVENESS DOESN'T ALWAYS SEEM EASY. If we feel attacked or hurt, we may try to relieve our pain by attacking the other person; we want them to know how much we're hurting. At such times, forgiveness may be far from our mind.

Forgiving someone can also feel like we're letting them off the hook, as in, "I know you did wrong, but I'm not going to punish you this time."

But true forgiveness is far from letting someone off, or even thinking they did wrong.

In the Bible the Greek word translated as "forgive" is *aphesis*. Its literal meaning is "to let go" — as when we physically let go of something, releasing our grip. With forgiveness, the grip we're releasing is a mental one. We're letting go of the judgments and grievances we've been holding against someone, along with our thoughts about how they should have behaved.

When someone doesn't behave as we expected or as we'd have liked them to, we may well feel angry. It's easy then to think the other person *made* us angry. We hold them responsible for our feelings.

However, on closer investigation, we usually find our anger comes not from their behavior but from how we have interpreted it — the story we are telling ourselves about what they've done and what they should have done. It would be more accurate to say we've made ourselves angry by how we judged the other person's behavior.

So when we forgive someone by letting go of our judgments about them, we actually help *ourselves* feel better. (In many cases, the other person may not know they have been forgiven — or even that we had been judging them.)

True forgiveness comes when we recognize that, deep down, the other person wants the same as us. In their own way, they are seeking to be at peace, to be free from pain and suffering.

This is not to imply that we should accept someone's bad behavior, or condone it. We may well feel the need to give feedback or make suggestions as to how they might behave better, but let's do so from a compassionate heart rather than a judgmental mind.

KINDNESS

THE WORD *kind* stems from *kin* — those of the same family or tribe, those we are close to — those of the same *kind*.

Deep down, we're all of the same kind. We want to be at ease, to be treated with respect, to feel cared for and appreciated. None of us wants to feel criticized, rejected, ignored, or manipulated. To reduce it to its simplest terms, we each want to feel loved. I don't mean love in a romantic sense, or some outpouring of emotion, but simple caring. This is the universal bottom line of every human relationship. We want to feel cared for. We want to be treated kindly.

If we ourselves want to be treated this way, we should do the same for others. But if we aren't careful, we easily end up doing the exact opposite. Instead of trying to ensure that someone feels cared for and appreciated, we can descend into a vicious circle of recrimination and attack.

It usually starts with feeling hurt over something that someone said or did. Whether or not they intended to hurt us doesn't matter. The fact is, we feel hurt. If we're not fully conscious of our emotional reactions, we might defend ourselves by attacking back. It's not the noblest or wisest response; nevertheless, it's the way we less-than-enlightened folk tend to react. It may be a cutting remark or criticism, a resentful tone of voice, a shift in body language, or simply a prolonged silence. Whatever form it takes, our underlying intention is for the other person to feel just a little hurt — not much, not enough to disrupt the relationship, but just enough that they don't feel totally loved.

But if, as is likely, the other person, too, is not fully aware of their emotional reactions, their response to a perceived attack will probably be similar to ours. They will attack back, doing or saying something intended to make us feel just a little hurt and not totally loved.

Soon a vicious circle gets set up. It may not always be that obvious. On the surface, the relationship might appear to be going well, with both parties appearing friendly and with no open hostility. But underneath a sad game is being played out. Each person, in their attempt to have the other behave in a more loving manner, is withholding their own love. They're effectively saying to each other, "You're not being kind to me. Therefore, I'm going to be a little unkind to you so that you realize the error of your ways and treat me better."

It's a lose-lose game. Little wonder many relationships — personal, social, and work — find themselves on rocky ground.

The vicious circle can be broken when we remember that, just as we want to feel loved and appreciated, so does the other person. Our intention then becomes: How can

I communicate so they don't feel attacked or rejected but cared for and respected?

We can start by becoming vigilant for our attacking thoughts and motives. Filtering out any attack, however subtle, from our communication can resolve much of the problem at its source.

This doesn't mean we shouldn't speak our truth. But we should explore ways to say it that help the other feel appreciated rather than attacked. When you have something difficult to say, you might preface it with the reason you want to say it, letting the other person know it comes from an attitude of caring rather than attack. For example, you might say, "I value our relationship and want to see it grow, but for that to happen, I need to discuss an issue that's difficult for me." This sets a very different tone from the one that might arise if you simply blurted it out.

Or it may help to express your own fears — they are also part of the truth. Revealing your fear of rejection, or of being misunderstood, can help the other appreciate your concerns and put them more at ease — which, remember, is the goal of this exercise.

And when this practice slips, as it surely will from time to time, and the attacking mode creeps back in, there's nothing like a genuine apology to set things back on track. Own up to your mistake (we're all human, after all), and try to express yourself again more caringly.

This practice of kindness is essentially the Golden Rule found at the heart of every religion. In the Bible it says, "Do unto others as you would have them do unto you." Similarly, in the Islamic tradition we find, "No one of you is a believer until he desires for his brother that which he desires for himself."

If we all applied this principle to everyone we met or spoke to, the world would be a very different place.

LOVING YOUR SELF

IT'S A COMMON REFRAIN: "Love yourself."

One way to interpret this is that you should love who you are, accept yourself just as you are, warts and all, having compassion for your shortfalls while rejoicing in your gifts. Loving ourselves in this way is certainly valuable; it can reduce self-judgment and free us to live more authentically.

Another way we can love ourselves is to take that feeling of love that dwells in our hearts, the feeling we know when we love someone, and let it flow toward our self — not loving anything in particular, just letting that feeling of love be there for ourself.

And there is another, deeper way of loving our self: loving what is sometimes called the "pure" or "true" self or simply the Self — that ever-present unchanging sense of I-ness at the heart of our being.

Most of the time, we don't notice this quiet inner presence. Our attention is focused on what we are thinking and experiencing. But when our attention relaxes and we drop back into our own being, we find an inner peace and ease, a great contentment to which nothing needs be added.

Knowing this essential nature is divine. Mystics have spoken volumes on it. Enlightened ones have urged us to open to it, to enjoy its calm, contented presence.

To rest in the Self is so delicious, we cannot help but love it.

It is what we've been longing for.

It is the beloved.

You are the Beloved.

LOVING LOVE

WE LOVE LOVE. It's one of our most basic needs, one we'll go to great lengths to meet.

But love is not something that comes to us or that we make happen. It is always alive in our being. It has been called "the secret sensation of the Self." A secret not because it is deliberately kept hidden but because our attention is usually so focused on our thoughts and experiences, we don't notice its presence. But when we rest in the Self we feel this love. We *are* love.

Love is accepting another's being, accepting them as they are. The opposite of love is nonacceptance — that is, judgment. Judgment arises from thinking that someone is not meeting our needs, values, or standards or is getting in the way of our search for happiness. All of which obscures our true nature.

Thus we find love by removing the veils to its presence. By letting go of judgment, letting go of control, letting go of fear — in short, by letting go of ego.

When we meet someone with whom we feel safe and

secure, allowing the ego-mind to let go, love reappears. We may think we've fallen in love with the person. But more accurately put, with them, we fall back into love.

We don't, however, have to wait for another person to provide the opportunity for us to return to love. When we sit quietly and let the thinking mind relax, we reconnect with our own being and with the essence of love.

There we can love love itself.

Savor how love feels. Soak in its soft warmth.

WISDOM

WHAT IS WISDOM? We hear the word a lot these days, as in the need for wisdom, wisdom traditions, wisdom schools, wisdom conferences.

Each of us would love to have more wisdom. And for others to have it, too. So much hurt and suffering comes from lack of wisdom. But what is this quality we hold in such high regard?

One way of looking at wisdom is in terms of the progression from data to information to knowledge.

Data are the raw facts, the letters on a page, for example.

Information comes from the patterns and structure in the data. Random letters provide little information, but if they spell words and the words create sentences, they carry information and meaning.

Knowledge comes with general conclusions we derive from collections of information — from reading a book, for example.

Wisdom concerns how we use this knowledge. Its

essence is discernment. Discernment of right from wrong. Helpful from harmful. Truth from delusion.

We may, for example, know that each of us wants to be happy, to be loved and appreciated. But do we use this knowledge to manipulate others for our own ends? Or do we use it to treat others with care and respect, helping them to feel happier and more content?

Those we regard as wise have discovered there's more to life than acquiring wealth and fame, that love and friendship count more than what others think of them. They are generally kind, content in themselves, able to discern their true self-interest.

There's a common perception that such wisdom comes with age. But why wait that long? In an ideal world, we would finish school not only with sufficient knowledge for the life ahead of us but also with the wisdom of how to use that knowledge.

The question then arises, Can we develop wisdom?

It turns out that the wisdom we seek is already there, at the heart of our being. Deep inside, we know right from wrong. But the quiet voice of our inner knowing is often obscured by the ego-mind, which has its own agenda of what is needed.

When we let go of ego and rest in the stillness of our essential being, the quiet voice of discernment can shine through as another way of seeing things.

DID BUDDHA HAVE IT EASY?

IN SOME RESPECTS, Buddha had it easy. He was not distracted by television, the internet, news of disasters in foreign lands, or the latest shenanigans of celebrities and politicians. He did not need to return phone calls, respond to emails piling up in his in-box, or catch up with the latest tweets and Facebook postings. He did not have to work at a job in order to pay the bills. He was not worried about stock market crashes, radiation leaks, climate change, or bank failures. He was not bombarded by seductive advertisements telling him he lacked this or that and could not be happy until he had it. He was not embedded in a culture that sought at every turn to engross his attention in unnecessary thoughts and distractions.

Yet his path was hard. The only spiritual advice he had as a young man was from traditional Vedic priests who advocated elaborate rituals and sacrifices as the path to salvation. He had to leave home and spend years wandering through the forests and villages of northern India, searching for spiritual guides. And those of any real help were few and far between; the spiritual pioneers of the time were just beginning to realize that spiritual liberation came from within rather than from a deity of some kind. He tried everything available, studying with the best teachers he could find, even adopting austerity to such a degree that he nearly died of starvation. But in the end, he had to work it out for himself. When he did, he came to the then radical realization that clinging to our ideas of how things should be causes suffering and keeps us apart from our true nature.

Today we have it so much easier. We can reap the benefit of Buddha's discoveries and those of his followers who have added their own realizations. And we can learn from a wealth of other spiritual traditions, from the mystics of all cultures, from native wisdom and other paths. We not only have the benefit of centuries of spiritual inquiry, but we can also access the wisdom of awakened people alive today. We can sit at their feet, read their words, listen to recordings, watch videos, or view livestreams on the internet. We also have advances in psychology, neuroscience, chemistry, and biology to augment our understanding and experience. Most significant, we are distilling the diverse expressions of this perennial wisdom into a common understanding. Stripping away the trappings of time and culture, we are collectively discovering that the essence of awakening is letting go of our preconceptions and judgments, returning our attention to the present moment, and recognizing our true nature.

On the one hand, with the wealth of teachers and teachings we have today, it is becoming easier and easier to awaken. On the other, the times we live in, with their incessant demands, make it ever more difficult. How do they balance out? Overall, is it easier or harder than it was 2,500 years ago? Who is to say? But we can shift the balance in our favor by taking advantage of the growing wealth of wisdom now so readily available, choosing the most effective and direct paths to waking up — while remaining mindful of the distractions of our contemporary world that make it so challenging to *stay* awake.

LETTING GO *to the* FUTURE

THERE'S SAID TO BE AN OLD CHINESE CURSE, "May you live in interesting times." Why is that a curse rather than a blessing? "Interesting times" implies there's a lot going on, much change afoot, new challenges to face. They may not, therefore, always be comfortable times.

Today's times are certainly interesting. On the one hand, advances in various fields are pushing the frontiers of knowledge and technology ahead ever faster. We have seen as much change in the past twenty years as we have in the previous hundred. Back in 2000, how many of us foresaw smartphones, social media, online shopping, and streaming movies? And we will probably see as much change again in the next *ten* years. Who knows what new technologies will then seem everyday?

On the other hand, humanity and the planet are facing unprecedented crises. Forests are dying fast. A growing number of species are becoming extinct. The air is hazed with pollution. Rivers run sour into the sea. Climate change has already brought extreme weather, crop failures, and flooded coastal regions, and may soon lead to mass migrations. Zoonotic diseases (those that cross from animals to humans) are appearing at a growing rate, making further pandemics increasingly likely.

Clearly, these are *not* comfortable times and are likely to become even less so. No one knows how it all will unfold, but whatever changes might come, the skill of letting go will be more important than ever.

Since change is coming ever faster, the future will be increasingly unpredictable. With events we can predict (for example, an impending hurricane), we have some idea of what will happen and how to prepare. But how do we prepare for the unexpected?

I like to draw an analogy with trees braving a storm. First, they need strong, firm roots so they won't blow over. Likewise, we should be firmly rooted in the ground of being. We'll need to remain cool, calm, and collected amid change, not thrown into fear or panic by every unexpected development. We'll need to let go of our beliefs about what will make us happy, remembering that what we are looking for in life — peace, ease, contentment — is available right here, within ourselves.

Like trees, which can sway with the wind, we, too, should be flexible. We'll need to let go of our ideas about how things should be and what the future might look like. Let go of expectations and our desire for certainty. And see things with fresh eyes rather than those of the past — a crucial element for the creative thinking and innovation that will be required of us.

Trees are safer in a forest than they are standing alone,

since they break the force of the wind for each other. Similarly, we fare better in community. The future is uncharted territory, and we'll feel vulnerable at times, needing to express our feelings or ask for emotional support, and at times material support. We will need to open our hearts and be more forgiving, remembering that, deep down, we all want the same: to be free from suffering, to feel respected and loved.

In a forest, a storm may be raging in the treetops while down on the ground all is still. So, too, we'll benefit from abiding in the stillness of our own being. Amid all the impermanence of life, this is one permanent place of refuge — the ever-present, unchanging quality of "I am," the calm center of our ever-turning world. There we can tap a source of wisdom and inspiration untainted by the agendas of ego-mind.

In short, we'll need to let go of whatever stands in the way of our being smarter, more creative, more resourceful, and more compassionate human beings, more in touch with our self, able to respond to change with greater clarity and wisdom.

And do so in whatever ways work for each of us. In these pages, I've suggested approaches that have helped me let go. You may well know others that help you. Good; the more the better.

I also know from experience how challenging it can be to stay on track. It's easy to get caught up in the many distractions the world has to offer, not to mention the many distractions our minds create for us.

Here again, community — helping each other on the

path, catching each other when we fall — is invaluable. Pointing out attachments we should let go of — whether to some possession, a story we are telling ourselves, some judgment, grievance, worry, or anything else that is creating unnecessary discontent. Reminding one another to relax, return to the present, and rest in the deep peace of our true nature.

The good news is, we are collectively homing in on the common core of the world's wisdom traditions, distilling their essence, and using previously unavailable media to share it around the world.

Moreover, we are doing so in everyday terms, bringing awakening down to earth — without metaphysical baggage, without being shrouded in the trappings of another culture or reserved for only a select few. Keeping it reasonable, simple, and understandable.

And, most important, we are making it attractive, something people desire — which takes us back to Ajahn Chah's words, which opened this book:

If you let go a little, you have a little peace.
If you let go a lot, you have a lot of peace.
If you let go completely, you have complete peace.

ABOUT *the* AUTHOR

PETER RUSSELL IS AN AUTHOR, speaker, and leading thinker on consciousness and contemporary spirituality. He believes the critical challenge today is freeing human thinking from the limited beliefs and attitudes that lie behind many of our problems — personal, social, and global. His mission is to distill the essential wisdom on human consciousness found in the world's various spiritual traditions and to disseminate it in contemporary and compelling ways. Russell earned a first-class honors degree in theoretical physics and psychology — as well as a master's degree in computer science — at the University of Cambridge, England. He also studied meditation and Eastern philosophy in India. He coined the term *global brain* with his 1980s bestseller by the same name, in which he predicted the internet and the impact it would have on humanity. He is the author of ten other books, including *Waking Up in Time* and *From Science to God.*

www.peterrussell.com

About Eckhart Tolle Editions

Eckhart Tolle Editions was launched in 2015 to publish life-changing works, both old and new, that have been personally selected by Eckhart Tolle. This imprint of New World Library presents books that can powerfully aid in transforming consciousness and awakening readers to a life of purpose and presence.

Learn more about Eckhart Tolle at

www.eckharttolle.com

NEW WORLD LIBRARY is dedicated to publishing books and other media that inspire and challenge us to improve the quality of our lives and the world.

We are a socially and environmentally aware company. We recognize that we have an ethical responsibility to our readers, our authors, our staff members, and our planet.

We serve our readers by creating the finest publications possible on personal growth, creativity, spirituality, wellness, and other areas of emerging importance. We serve our authors by working with them to produce and promote quality books that reach a wide audience. We serve New World Library employees with generous benefits, significant profit sharing, and constant encouragement to pursue their most expansive dreams.

Whenever possible, we print our books with soy-based ink on 100 percent postconsumer-waste recycled paper. We power our offices with solar energy and contribute to nonprofit organizations working to make the world a better place for us all.

Our products are available wherever books are sold. Visit our website to download our catalog, subscribe to our e-newsletter, read our blog, and link to authors' websites, videos, and podcasts.

customerservice@newworldlibrary.com

Phone: 415-884-2100 or 800-972-6657

Orders: Ext. 110 • Catalog requests: Ext. 110

Fax: 415-884-2199

www.newworldlibrary.com